Describing the Indescribable

DESCRIBING THE INDESCRIBABLE

A Commentary on the Diamond Sutra

by Master Hsing Yun

translated by Tom Graham

Wisdom Publications
199 Elm Street
Somerville, MA 02144
wisdompubs.org

Library of Congress Cataloging-in-Publication Data
Xingyundashi.
      Describing the indescribable : a commentary on the Diamond Sutra/by Master
Hsing Yun ; translated by Tom Graham
      p.   cm.
      Includes the translation of the Diamond Sutra.
      Includes bibliographical references.
      ISBN 0-86171-186-6 (alk. paper)
      I. Tripi̱aka. Sūtrapiṭaka. Prajñāpāramitā. Vajracchedikā—Criticism, interpreta-
tion, etc. I. Graham, Tom. II. Tripitaka. Sutrapitaka. Prajñaparamita. Vajracchedika
English. III. Title

BQ1997.X46 2000
294.3'85—dc21   00-054080

ISBN 978-0-86171-186-4   ebook ISBN 978-0-86171-826-9
20 19 18 17 16
 6 5 4 2

Cover and interior design by Gopa&Ted2, Inc. Set in Adobe Garamond 11 pt./13 pt.
Cover image: Chinese Wood cut AD 868. The Buddha discoursing to Subhuti. The Chinese Translation Diamond Sutra. © 19th era / Alamy Stock Photo.

Wisdom Publications' books are printed on acid-free paper and meet the guidelines
for permanence and durability of the Production Guidelines for Book Longevity of the
Council on Library Resources.

🏵 This book was produced with environmental mindfulness.
For more information, please visit wisdompubs.org/wisdom-environment.

Printed in the United States of America.

Contents

Translator's Preface

The Buddha was a great communicator. He never hid his meaning or tried to confuse his listeners. Buddhist sutras, which are records of talks given by the Buddha, are models of clarity, insight, and intelligence. The Chinese translation of the *Diamond Sutra*, on which this commentary is based, is revered in East Asia largely because it possesses an uncanny clarity that almost makes us see through time to the Jeta Grove where the Buddha gave this famous talk.

Kumarajiva (344–413), who made the Chinese translation in 401 C.E., must have felt a very deep sense of responsibility, for though his translation is considered to be one of China's great works of literature, he is said to have commented while reading it afterward that it was so uninspired it was like "chewing on chips of wood." Indeed, his translation may really have sounded that way in 401 C.E. in Chang An, China. Time has a way of making great works of literature even greater because one generation after another studies them and absorbs them into the language they use. The Chinese language curls around Kumarajiva's translation of the *Diamond Sutra* the way the English language curls around the works of Shakespeare or Chaucer. Kumarajiva established a vocabulary and a manner of expression that is echoed in almost all other Chinese Buddhist writings. As the Buddha surely would have wanted, his work is marked by its clarity, its economy of style, and its elegance.

Kumarajiva, who was of Central Asian origin, and who was as much influenced by Kashmir as he was by China, set a tone for Chinese

Buddhism that has prevailed to this day. This tone, coupled with the visual beauty of the Chinese language, easily makes Buddhist literature in Chinese one of the world's most satisfying spiritual and intellectual traditions. Master Hsing Yun is an important modern exponent of this tradition. His life and his writings have been one of the main forces in the revitalization of Chinese Buddhism in the world today. His monastery in Taiwan is the largest Chinese Buddhist monastery in the world.

Needless to say, the job of translating his work into English is not easy, especially when that work is a commentary on a sutra that was translated from the Sanskrit by Kumarajiva. Two very influential writers separated by sixteen centuries meet in a single volume, wherein one comments at length on the work of the other. Strictly speaking this is a translation that cannot be made. But Buddhism is a profound spiritual tradition based on principles deeper than the surface features of any language or even language itself. Indeed, the wisdom teachings of the Buddha, of which the *Diamond Sutra* is a part, state very clearly that the meaning of the Buddha's teaching must always be considered on three different levels. The first is the surface level of words, the second is the meaning of the words, and the third and most important level is the deep import of the words—the oceanic depths of the Buddha's teaching that have the power to change who we are and how we interpret our worlds.

The difficulty of translating both the commentary and the sutra forced me to search for this deeper level wherever I could, and thus I sometimes had to adjust the first and second levels of meaning to fit the English language. To do this most effectively, I did not rely exclusively on Master Hsing Yun's commentary on the sutra, but consulted all of his works—including oral teachings—to try to forge an explication of the sutra that is true to Master Hsing Yun's deepest sensibilities as well as to the deepest meaning of the sutra. This approach has the full blessing and encouragement of Master Hsing Yun, for he understands, perhaps better than anyone, that a tentative touch, or one that is too bound up in Chinese culture, will never succeed in bringing this sutra alive for readers of English. Thus notes that once referred to idiosyncrasies of the Chinese language now may refer to idiosyncrasies of the English language, and commentary that depends on responses peculiar to a Chinese readership may now depend on responses peculiar to readers of English.

To make the commentary correspond to the sutra, I had to retranslate the sutra itself. Though several good translations of the *Diamond Sutra* already exist in English, they tend to be interpretive and to use vocabulary that drifts quite far from the Chinese. The translation of the sutra included in this volume is nearly literal. It is my hope that this will allow the commentary, which so often refers to the basic meanings of words, to make much better sense to readers of English. The notes section at the end of this volume is an integral part of the original commentary. These notes should serve to deepen appreciation of both the sutra and Master Hsing Yun's discussion of it.

Some people may wonder if a translation and commentary on the *Diamond Sutra* can be complete without including references to Sanskrit versions of the sutra. The answer to this is twofold. Firstly, Master Hsing Yun's commentary, as with most Chinese commentaries on the sutra, does not refer to a Sanskrit version. And secondly, Kumarajiva's translation into Chinese is the oldest reliable version of the sutra now extant.

The Sanskrit meanings of many words are discussed in the commentary, but these discussions are based not on a Sanskrit version of this sutra, but on the ways that these words are understood within the tradition of Chinese Buddhism. These discussions are part of the first two levels of meaning that the Buddha said were necessary to get to the third and deepest level of his teachings. The effort put into understanding how the Buddha used words and why he chose the ones he did will be repaid many times, for his use of language cuts to the very core of human awareness, as it opens before us vistas that expand beyond anything we may have experienced before.

I would like to thank Master Hsing Yun and members of Buddha's Light International Association for their support for this translation. I would also like to thank Ven. Yi Jih, without whose help this work would not have been possible. My deep thanks also to Ven. Miao Jie, Ananda W. P. Guruge, Sandra Wawrytko, David Kittelstrom, Jeff Jenkins,

Emily Hague, Carl Ewig, Robert Jones, and Maryrita Hillengas for their valuable help and encouragement.

May all merit that may accrue from this work be shared by sentient beings everywhere.

Tom Graham
San Diego, California

Introduction

Historically, Chinese Buddhism has been influenced by two streams of thought. One stream is concerned with karma, rebirth, and the many factors that condition our lives, while the other is concerned with the Buddha's teachings on wisdom and emptiness. The first stream explains life in this world and the things that condition it, while the second stream teaches us how to comprehend the mind of a buddha.

The Buddha's teachings on wisdom and emptiness are usually called his *prajna* teachings. *Prajna* is a Sanskrit word meaning "wisdom" or "discernment." There is a great deal of variety in Chinese prajna literature because the sutras and commentaries concerning it entered China at several different times and places; in addition to this, there are usually several translations into Chinese of each of these different works. Without question, the *Diamond Sutra* is the single best representative we have of the Buddha's prajna teachings. It is a small gem of great value, for to understand the *Diamond Sutra* is to understand the enlightened mind of the Buddha himself. *The Diamond Sutra* is the quintessence of the Buddha's teachings on wisdom. Though it is quite short, no other sutra or commentary within the prajna tradition has been discussed or written about more than the *Diamond Sutra*.

My goal for this book is to provide readers with the core of the Buddha's teachings on wisdom. I have drawn on the writings of several commentators, and particularly on those of Master P'u Wan, who lived during the early years of the Ch'ing Dynasty (1644–1911). Prince Chao

Ming's (499–529) division of the sutra into thirty-two sections is the traditional division used in China, and I have followed this tradition.

The *Diamond Sutra* beats with two hearts: one is wisdom and the other is compassion. To be wise is to know and understand the essence of awareness. To be compassionate is to know and understand the essence of intention. In the *Diamond Sutra*, the Buddha shows us that ultimately compassion and wisdom are one. When this is fully understood, we will have understood the *Diamond Sutra*. When this is fully understood, we will know on what to "base our minds," and we will also know that in truth there are no defilements "to be subdued."

I hope that the reader will derive a profound and lasting comfort from the *Diamond Sutra*. It presents the single greatest solution that I know of to the trials and tribulations of life. The *Diamond Sutra* describes the very foundation of conscious life.

I know both that my understanding of the *Diamond Sutra* is flawed and that my ability to explain it to others is limited. Nevertheless, I hope that my words will in some small way lead the reader to understand what the Buddha meant by prajna. Prajna is sometimes called the "mother of all buddhas" because it elucidates the very nature of consciousness. The pure wisdom described in the *Diamond Sutra* has the power to carry us beyond life and death to the ultimate bliss of nirvana.

Master Hsing Yun

The Diamond Sutra

The Diamond Sutra

1. The Causes of This Dharma Meeting

Thus have I heard. At one time, the Buddha was in the state of Shravasti at the Jeta Grove with a gathering of monks numbering 1,250. At mealtime, the World-honored One put on his robe, picked up his bowl, and went into the city of Shravasti to beg for food. After he had gone from house to house, he returned to the grove. When he had finished eating, he put away his robe and bowl, washed his feet, straightened his mat, and sat down.

2. Subhuti's Request

At that time the elder monk Subhuti was among the gathering of monks. He rose from his seat, bared his right shoulder, kneeled on his right knee, and with palms pressed together before him, respectfully spoke to the Buddha saying, "Rare One, World-honored One, the Tathagata protects and is concerned about all bodhisattvas, and he instructs all bodhisattvas. World-honored One, when good men and good women commit themselves to highest complete enlightenment, on what should they base themselves, and how should they subdue their minds?"

The Buddha said, "Wonderful! Wonderful! Subhuti, you said that the Tathagata protects and is concerned about all bodhisattvas, and that he instructs all bodhisattvas. Now listen carefully while I tell you, when good men and good women commit themselves to highest complete enlightenment, on what they should base themselves, and how they should subdue their minds."

"Excellent, World-honored One. I eagerly await your answer."

3. The Heart of the Mahayana

The Buddha said to Subhuti, "All great bodhisattvas should subdue their minds in the following manner: they should realize as they vow to save all sentient beings that in truth there are no sentient beings to be saved. And they should realize as they vow to save all of the infinite, innumerable, illimitable sentient beings that in reality there are no sentient beings to be saved. When they vow to lead them all to nirvana without remainder—be they born of eggs, wombs, moisture, or transformation, or whether they have form, or no form, or whether they are able to perceive, or do not perceive, or cannot perceive, or will not perceive—they should realize that in truth there are no sentient beings to be led to nirvana.

"And why is this? Subhuti, if a bodhisattva has *lakshana* of self, lakshana of human beings, lakshana of sentient beings, or lakshana of a soul, then he is not a bodhisattva."

4. The Wonder of Behaving Without Attachment

"Moreover, Subhuti, within this phenomenal world, a bodhisattva ought to practice generosity without basing it on anything.

This means that he should not base his generosity on form, and he should not base his generosity on sound, smell, taste, touch, or thought. Subhuti, the generosity of a bodhisattva should be like this and should not be based on any lakshana whatsoever. And why is this? If the generosity of a bodhisattva is not based on any lakshana whatsoever, then his goodness will be immeasurable.

"Subhuti, what do you say, can the vastness of space to the east of us be measured?"

"No, it cannot, World-honored One."

"Subhuti, can the vastness of space in any direction be measured? Can the vastness of space to the south, west, north, up, or down be measured?"

"No, it cannot, World-honored One."

"Subhuti, when the generosity of a bodhisattva is not based on lakshana, his goodness is just as immeasurable as that. Subhuti, a bodhisattva should base himself on this teaching and this teaching alone."

5. Seeing the Truth That Lies Beneath Perception

"Subhuti, what do you say, can you see the Tathagata in his bodily lakshana?"

"No, World-honored One, no one can see the Tathagata in his bodily lakshana. And why is this? The bodily lakshana that the Tathagata is talking about are not bodily lakshana."

The Buddha said to Subhuti, "All lakshana are delusive. If you can see that all lakshana are not lakshana, then you will see the Tathagata."

6. The Rarity of True Belief

Subhuti said to the Buddha, "World-honored One, can sentient beings, upon hearing these words, really be expected to believe them?"

The Buddha told Subhuti, "Don't talk like that. Even after I have been gone for five hundred years, there will still be people who are moral and who cultivate goodness. If they can believe this teaching and accept it as the truth, you can be sure that they will have planted good roots not just with one buddha, or two buddhas, or three, or four, or five buddhas, but that they will have planted good roots with tens of millions of buddhas. And if someone has so much as a single pure moment of belief concerning this teaching, Subhuti, they will be intimately known and seen by the Tathagata. And what is the reason that these sentient beings will attain such infinite goodness? These sentient beings will not return to the lakshana of self, the lakshana of human beings, the lakshana of sentient beings, the lakshana of souls, the lakshana of laws, or the lakshana of non-laws.

"And why is this? If a sentient being clings to lakshana in his mind, then he will cling to self, human beings, sentient beings, or souls. If he clings to the lakshana of a law, then he will also cling to self, human beings, sentient beings, or souls. And why is this? If he clings to even so little as the lakshana of a non-law, then he will also cling to self, human beings, sentient beings, or souls. Thus, he must not cling to laws or non-laws, and this is why I have often said to you monks that even my teachings should be understood to be like a raft; if even the Dharma must be let go of, then how much more must everything else be let go of?"

7. Nothing Has Been Attained and Nothing Has Been Said

"Subhuti, what do you say? Has the Tathagata really attained highest complete enlightenment? Has the Tathagata really spoken a dharma?"

Subhuti said, "As far as I understand what the Buddha has said, there is no definite dharma that can be called highest complete enlightenment, and there is no definite dharma that could be spoken about by the Tathagata. And why is this? The Dharma of which the Tathagata speaks cannot be held onto, it cannot be spoken, it is not a law, and it is not a non-law. And that is why all bodhisattvas understand the unconditioned dharmas differently."

8. Enlightenment Comes from These Teachings

"Subhuti, what do you say? If a person, in an act of generosity, were to give away enough precious jewels to fill an entire great chiliocosm, would the goodness he achieved be great or not?"

Subhuti said, "It would be very great, World-honored One. And why is this? This goodness is devoid of a 'goodness nature,' and therefore the Tathagata would say that it is great."

"If someone else were to receive and uphold as few as four verses of this sutra, and if he were to teach them to others, his goodness would be even greater than that. And why is this? Subhuti, all buddhas and all highest complete enlightenment are born of this sutra. Subhuti, that which is called the Buddhadharma is not the Buddhadharma."

9. The Four Fruits Are Empty

"Subhuti, what do you say? Would it be right for a *shrotapana* to think like this: 'I have attained the fruit of a shrotapana'?"

Subhuti said, "No, World-honored One. And why is this? *Shrotapana* means 'stream-enterer,' and yet there is nothing to be entered. Indeed, to not enter into form, sound, smell, taste, touch, or thought is what is called shrotapana."

"Subhuti, what do you say? Would it be right for a *sakradagami* to think like this: 'I have attained the fruit of a sakradagami'?"

Subhuti said, "No, World-honored One. And why is this? *Sakradagami* means 'once-returner,' and yet in truth there is no such thing as returning. This is what is called sakradagami."

"Subhuti, what do you say? Would it be right for an *anagami* to think like this: 'I have attained the fruit of an anagami'?"

Subhuti said, "No, World-honored One. And why is this? *Anagami* means 'never-returner,' and yet in truth there is no such thing as never returning. This is the reason it is called anagami."

"Subhuti, what do you say? Would it be right for an *arahant* to think like this: 'I have attained the path of an arahant'?"

Subhuti said, "No, World-honored One. And why is this? There is no dharma called 'arahant.' World-honored One, if an arahant were to think 'I have attained the path of an arahant,' then he would be clinging to self, human being, sentient being, and soul.

"World-honored One, the Buddha has said that I have attained nondisputational *samadhi*, and that among all people, I am the best in this; and that among all arahants, I am also the best at going beyond desire. And yet, I do not have the thought that I am an arahant that has gone beyond desire. World-honored One, if I were to have the thought that I had attained the path of an arahant, then the World-honored One would not have said that Subhuti takes delight in the practice of *aranya*. Since Subhuti is wholly without any practice, Subhuti has been said to take delight in the practice of aranya."

10. Making the Buddha Realm Magnificent

The Buddha said to Subhuti, "What do you say? When the Tathagata was in the realm of Dipankara Buddha, did he gain anything by his practice of the Dharma?"

"No, World-honored One, when the Tathagata was in the realm of Dipankara Buddha, he did not gain anything from his practice of the Dharma."

"Subhuti, what do you say? Does a bodhisattva make a buddha realm magnificent?"

"No, World-honored One. And why is this? That which makes a buddha realm magnificent is not magnificent, and this is what is called magnificence."

"For this reason, Subhuti, all great bodhisattvas should give rise to purity of mind in this way: they should give rise to a mind that is not based on form, and they should give rise to a mind that is not based on sound, smell, taste, touch, or thought. They should give rise to a mind that is not based on anything.

"Subhuti, what do you say? If a man's body were as large as Mount Sumeru, would that body be large?"

Subhuti said, "Very large, World-honored One. And why is this? The Buddha has said that no body is what is called the large body."

11. The Unconditioned Is Supreme

"Subhuti, if each grain of sand in the Ganges River were to become a Ganges River, and if the sand in all of those rivers were added up, what do you say? Would that be a lot of sand?"

Subhuti said, "It would be very much, World-honored One. The number of Ganges Rivers alone would be enormous; the amount of sand would be even greater than that."

"Subhuti, I am going to speak the truth to you now: if a good man or a good woman were to give away as many great chiliocosms of precious jewels as all of those grains of sand, would his goodness be great?"

Subhuti said, "It would be very great, World-honored One."

The Buddha said to Subhuti, "If a good man or a good woman receives and upholds as few as four verses of this sutra, and if he teaches them to others, then his goodness will be greater than that."

12. Honoring the True Teaching

"Furthermore, Subhuti, anyone who speaks about this sutra, even as little as only four verses of it, should be honored by people in this world, by those in heaven, and by *ashuras* as if he were a Buddhist shrine. And anyone who practices the teachings of this sutra with all of his strength, or who reads it, or chants it, should be honored that much more. Subhuti, you should know that such a person already has become accomplished in the highest and rarest of dharmas. Wherever this sutra can be found, there also is the Buddha; and it should be honored as if it were one of his disciples."

13. The Name of This Sutra

At that point, Subhuti asked the Buddha, "World-honored One, what should this sutra be called, and how should we receive it and uphold it?"

The Buddha said to Subhuti, "This sutra is called the *Diamond Prajnaparamita*, and by this name you should receive it and uphold it. And why is this? Subhuti, the Buddha has said that the perfection of wisdom is not the perfection of wisdom and that that is what is called the perfection of wisdom. Subhuti, what do you say? Does the Tathagata really have some dharma to speak about?"

Subhuti said to the Buddha, "World-honored One, the Tathagata has nothing to speak about."

"Subhuti, what do you say? Is the fine dust of an entire great chiliocosm a lot of dust or not?"

Subhuti said, "It is a lot, World-honored One."

"Subhuti, the Tathagata says that all of that fine dust is not fine dust, and that that is what is called fine dust. The Tathagata says that the world is not the world, and that that is what is called the world. Subhuti, what do you say? Can the Tathagata be seen by his thirty-two marks?"

"No, World-honored One. And why is this? The Tathagata has said that the thirty-two marks are not marks, and that that is what is called thirty-two marks."

"Subhuti, if a good man or a good woman were to practice generosity with as many lives as there are grains of sand in the Ganges River, his or her goodness would still not be as great as that of someone who upheld as few as four verses of this sutra and who spoke of them to others."

14. Ultimate Tranquility Beyond Lakshana

Then, after hearing this sutra and comprehending its deep meaning, Subhuti wept out loud and said to the Buddha, "Rare One,
World-honored One, of all the wise things that I have ever heard,
I have never heard anything as profound as the sutra that the Buddha has just spoken. World-honored One, if anyone should hear
this sutra and believe it with a pure mind, then he will give rise to
the true lakshana, and he will attain supreme goodness of the rarest
kind. World-honored One, the true lakshana is not a lakshana,
and that is why the Tathagata has called it a true lakshana.

"World-honored One, today I have heard this sutra, believed it,
understood it, received it, and upheld it, and this was not diycult.
If five hundred years from now, someone should hear this sutra,
believe it, understand it, receive it, and uphold it, then that person
will be a rare person indeed. And why is this? That person will be
without lakshana of self, lakshana of human beings, lakshana of
sentient beings, or lakshana of a soul. And why is this? Lakshana
of self are not lakshana, and lakshana of human beings, sentient
beings, or souls are not lakshana. And why is this? That which is
disentangled from all lakshana is called all buddhas."

The Buddha said to Subhuti, "Just so, just so. Moreover, if a person hears this sutra and does not become alarmed, or frightened, or
scared, then this person is indeed a rare person. And why is this?
Subhuti, the Tathagata has said that the supreme *paramita* is not
the supreme paramita, and that this is what is called the supreme
paramita. Subhuti, the Tathagata has said that the paramita of
patience under insult is not the paramita of patience under insult.
And why is this? Subhuti, long ago when my body was being cut
apart by Kalingaraja, I had no lakshana of a self, no lakshana of
human beings, no lakshana of sentient beings, and no lakshana of

a soul. And why was this? If at that distant time, as my body was being cut apart piece by piece, if I had had lakshana of self, lakshana of human beings, lakshana of sentient beings, or lakshana of a soul, I would have become angry. Subhuti, think about this some more; five hundred generations ago when I was patient under insult, I was without lakshana of self, lakshana of human beings, lakshana of sentient beings, or lakshana of a soul. For this reason, Subhuti, a bodhisattva should disentangle himself from all lakshana, and commit himself to highest complete enlightenment; and he should not give rise to a mind based on form, and he should not give rise to a mind based on sound, smell, taste, touch, or thought. He should give rise to a mind that is not based on anything. Even if the mind is based on something, it is not really based on anything, and for this reason the Buddha says that the generosity of a bodhisattva should not be based on form. Subhuti, a bodhisattva should be generous in this way for the purpose of aiding all sentient beings. The Tathagata says that all lakshana are not lakshana, and therefore he also says that all sentient beings are not sentient beings.

"Subhuti, the Tathagata is one of real words, truthful words, correct words, not false words, and not one who changes his words. Subhuti, the Dharma that the Tathagata has attained is not true and it is not false.

"Subhuti, when a bodhisattva bases his mind on some dharma and then acts generously, he is like a person who has entered into darkness—he sees nothing at all. But when a bodhisattva does not base his mind on any dharma and then acts generously, he is like someone who has eyes in the full light of the sun—he sees all forms clearly.

"Subhuti, if in future generations there are good men and good women who can practice this sutra, and read it, and chant it, then the Tathagata in his buddha wisdom will intimately know and intimately see those people, and they will attain complete, limitless, and boundless goodness."

15. The Goodness of Upholding This Sutra

"Subhuti, even if a good man or a good woman were generous in the morning with as many bodies as there are grains of sand in the Ganges River, and even if this generosity were repeated at midday with as many bodies as there are grains of sand in the Ganges River, and even if this generosity were repeated at night with as many bodies as there are grains of sand in the Ganges River, and even if all of this generosity were continued for an immense number of eons, still his or her goodness would not be as great as that of another person who heard this sutra, who believed it, and who did not go against it. And if this is so, imagine how much greater is the goodness of one who copies this sutra, practices it, reads it, chants it, and explains it to others. Subhuti, the most important thing that can be said about this sutra is that its goodness is inconceivable, immeasurable, and boundless. The Tathagata speaks this sutra to those who have committed themselves to the Great Vehicle; he speaks it to those who have committed themselves to the Supreme Vehicle. Those who uphold this sutra, and read it, and chant it, and explain it to others, will be intimately known and intimately seen by the Tathagata. All such people will attain to a goodness that is immeasurable, unlimited, boundless, and inconceivable. And all such people will share in the highest complete enlightenment of the Tathagata. And why is this? Subhuti, those who delight in lower dharmas cling to a view of a self, a view of human beings, a view of sentient beings, and a view of a soul, and thus they are not able to listen to this sutra, to receive it, to read it, to chant it, or to explain it to others. Subhuti, in whatever place this sutra can be found, it should be honored by all who are in this world, and all in heaven, and all ashuras. They should treat this place as if it were a shrine; they should surround it, bow to it, and pay their deepest respects to it. They should scatter incense and flowers all around this place."

16. Purification of Karma

"Furthermore, Subhuti, if a good man or good woman is slighted or ridiculed by others for upholding, reading, or chanting this sutra, it is due to bad karma incurred in a former life. That bad karma should be the cause of the person falling into a lower realm, but in this life he is just being slighted and ridiculed. Eventually his bad karma from previous lives will be eradicated, and he will attain highest complete enlightenment.

"Subhuti, I remember countless eons ago, when I was before Dipankara Buddha, I met, honored, and made overings to all of the countless buddhas in the universe without excepting a single one of them. If someone in the Dharma-declining age can practice, read, and chant this sutra, the goodness he will attain will be a hundred times—nay, a billion billion times, nay, an incalculable number of times that cannot even be suggested by metaphors—greater than the goodness I attained for honoring all buddhas.

"Subhuti, if I were to say completely how great is the goodness attained by a good man or a good woman who practices, reads, and chants this sutra in the Dharma-declining age, there would be those whose minds would become crazy upon hearing this, and they would form deep doubts and not believe it. Subhuti, it is enough to know that this sutra is inconceivably great and that the rewards it overs are inconceivably great."

17. Complete and Utter Selflessness

Then Subhuti asked the Buddha, "World-honored One, when good men and good women commit themselves to highest complete enlightenment, on what should they base themselves? And how should they subdue their minds?"

The Buddha said to Subhuti, "When good men and good women commit themselves to highest complete enlightenment, they should give rise to a mind like this: 'I should save all sentient beings, and as I save them, I should know that there really are no sentient beings to be saved.' And why is this? If a bodhisattva has lakshana of self, lakshana of human beings, lakshana of sentient beings, or lakshana of a soul, then he is not a bodhisattva. And why is this? Subhuti, in truth, there is no such dharma as committing to highest complete enlightenment.

"Subhuti, what do you say? When the Tathagata was in the realm of Dipankara Buddha, was there an attainable dharma 'highest complete enlightenment' or not?"

"There was not, World-honored One. As far as I understand the meaning of what the Buddha has said, when the Buddha was in the realm of Dipankara Buddha, there was no attainable dharma 'highest complete enlightenment.'"

The Buddha said, "Just so, just so. Subhuti, in truth, there is no dharma 'highest complete enlightenment' for the Tathagata to attain. Subhuti, if the Tathagata had attained a dharma 'highest complete enlightenment,' then Dipankara Buddha would never have told me, 'In the future you will attain buddhahood and be called Shakyamuni.' Since there is no attainable dharma 'highest complete enlightenment,' Dipankara Buddha told me that I would become a buddha, saying, 'In the future you will attain buddhahood and be called Shakyamuni.' And why is this? The Tathagata is the essence of all dharmas. Someone might say,

'The Tathagata has attained highest complete enlightenment,' but Subhuti, there really is no dharma 'highest complete enlightenment' for the Buddha to attain. Subhuti, the highest complete enlightenment that the Tathagata has attained lies between these two and is neither true nor false.

"For these reasons, the Tathagata says that all dharmas are the Buddhadharma. Subhuti, that which is said to be all dharmas is not all dharmas, and that is why it is called all dharmas. Subhuti, it is the same as a person growing up."

Subhuti said, "World-honored One, the Tathagata has said that when a person grows up, he has not grown up, and that this is what is meant by growing up."

"Subhuti, a bodhisattva is just like that, and if he should say, 'I should save all sentient beings,' then he is not a bodhisattva. And why is this? Subhuti, there is no dharma called 'bodhisattva,' and for this reason the Buddha has said that all dharmas have no self, no human being, no sentient being, and no soul. Subhuti, if a bodhisattva should say, 'I make the buddha realm magnificent,' then he is not a bodhisattva. And why is this? The Tathagata has said that that which makes the buddha realm magnificent is not magnificent, and that that is what is called magnificence. Subhuti, only after a bodhisattva has fully understood the dharma of selflessness will the Tathagata say that he is a true bodhisattva."

18. One Body Sees All

"Subhuti, what do you say, does the Tathagata have eyes of flesh or not?"

"Yes, World-honored One, the Tathagata has eyes of flesh."

"Subhuti, what do you say, does the Tathagata have heavenly eyes or not?"

"Yes, World-honored One, the Tathagata has heavenly eyes."

"Subhuti, what do you say, does the Tathagata have wisdom eyes or not?"

"Yes, World-honored One, the Tathagata has wisdom eyes."

"Subhuti, what do you say, does the Tathagata have Dharma eyes or not?"

"Yes, World-honored One, the Tathagata has Dharma eyes."

"Subhuti, what do you say, does the Tathagata have buddha eyes or not?"

"Yes, World-honored One, the Tathagata has buddha eyes."

"Subhuti, what do you say, has the Buddha said that the sand in the Ganges River is sand or not?"

"Yes, World-honored One, the Tathagata has said that it is sand."

"Subhuti, what do you say, if there were as many Ganges Rivers as there are grains of sand in the Ganges River, and if all of the sand of all of those rivers were added up, and if the number of buddha realms equaled the number of all of those grains of sand, would that be a lot?"

"It would be very much, World-honored One."

The Buddha said to Subhuti, "The Tathagata intimately knows each and every sentient being in all of those worlds. And how can this be? The Tathagata has said that all minds are not minds and that that is what is called mind. And why is this so? Subhuti, the mind of the past cannot be gotten hold of, the mind of the present cannot be gotten hold of, and the mind of the future cannot be gotten hold of."

19. Universal Transformation Within the Dharma Realm

"Subhuti, what do you say? If a person gives away enough precious jewels to fill an entire great chiliocosm, will this cause him to attain immense goodness?"

"Just so, World-honored One. This will cause him to attain immense goodness."

"Subhuti, if there really were such a thing as goodness, the Tathagata would never speak about attaining immense goodness. It is only because there is no such thing as goodness that the Tathagata says that immense goodness can be attained."

20. Beyond Form and Lakshana

"Subhuti, what do you say? Can the Buddha be seen in his complete form body or not?"

"No, World-honored One, the Buddha ought not to be seen in his form body. And why is this? The Tathagata has said that his complete form body is not the complete form body, and that this is what is called the complete form body."

"Subhuti, what do you say? Can the Tathagata be seen by means of all complete lakshana or not?"

"No, World-honored One. The Tathagata ought not to be seen by means of all complete lakshana. And why is this? The Tathagata has said that the completeness of all lakshana is not completeness and that this is what is called completeness of all lakshana."

21. *Speaking the Unspeakable*

"Subhuti, never say that the Tathagata has this thought: 'I have some dharma to speak about.' Do not have that thought. And why is this? If someone says that the Tathagata has a dharma to speak about, then that person is defaming the Buddha, and he does not understand what I have been saying. Subhuti, one who speaks the Dharma has no Dharma to speak about and that is what is called speaking the Dharma."

Then the wise Subhuti said to the Buddha, "World-honored One, will there ever be sentient beings in the future who upon hearing this Dharma will give rise to believing minds?"

The Buddha said, "Subhuti, those sentient beings are not sentient beings, and they are not not sentient beings. And why is this? Subhuti, the Tathagata has said that all sentient beings are not sentient beings and that this is what is called sentient beings."

22. *The Unattainable Dharma*

Subhuti said to the Buddha, "World-honored One, is it not so that when the Buddha attained highest complete enlightenment, nothing was really attained?"

"Just so, just so. Subhuti, there is not even the slightest dharma that can be attained in highest complete enlightenment, and this is what is called highest complete enlightenment."

23. *Perfect Equanimity*

"Furthermore, Subhuti, this dharma is equal and without high or low; it is called highest complete enlightenment. Highest complete enlightenment is attained by cultivating all good dharmas while being without self, without human being, without sentient being, and without soul. Subhuti, when I say 'all good dharmas,' the Tathagata is saying that not all good dharmas is what is called all good dharmas."

24. True Generosity Lies in Upholding This Sutra

"Subhuti, if a person were to perform an act of generosity by giving away a quantity of precious jewels equal to all of the Sumeru mountains within a great chiliocosm; and if another person were to uphold as few as four verses of this Prajnaparamita Sutra, and read them, and chant them, and explain them to others, the goodness of this second person would be a hundred times—nay, a billion billion times, nay, an incalculable number of times that cannot even be suggested by metaphors—greater than the goodness of the first person."

25. Transforming That Which Cannot Be Transformed

"Subhuti, what do you say? Don't you ever say that the Tathagata has this thought: 'I am saving sentient beings.' Subhuti, don't have this thought. And why is this? In truth, there are no sentient beings for the Tathagata to save. If there were sentient beings for the Tathagata to save, then the Tathagata would have lakshana of self, human being, sentient being, and soul.

"Subhuti, when the Tathagata speaks of a self, it is the same as no self, and yet all ordinary people take it as a self. Subhuti, the Tathagata says that ordinary people are not ordinary people, and that this is what is called ordinary people."

26. The Dharma Body Is Without Lakshana

"Subhuti, what do you say? Can the Tathagata be seen by his thirty-two marks or not?"

Subhuti said, "Just so, just so. The Tathagata can be seen by his thirty-two marks."

The Buddha said, "Subhuti, if the Tathagata could be seen by his thirty-two marks, then a wheel-turning sage-king would be the same as the Tathagata."

Subhuti said to the Buddha, "World-honored One, as far as I understand the meaning of what the Buddha has said, one ought not to be able to see the Tathagata by his thirty-two marks."

Then the Buddha spoke a verse:

> If anyone should think that I can be seen among forms,
> Or that I can be sought among sounds,
> Then that person is on the wrong path
> And he will not see the Tathagata.

27. Nothing Is Ended and Nothing Is Extinguished

"Subhuti, consider this thought: 'The Tathagata attains highest complete enlightenment because his lakshana are incomplete.' Subhuti, do not have this thought: 'The Tathagata attains highest complete enlightenment because his lakshana are incomplete.'

"Subhuti, consider this thought: 'The one who commits to highest complete enlightenment says that all dharmas are ended and extinguished.' Do not have this thought. And why is this? The one who commits to highest complete enlightenment does not say that lakshana are ended and extinguished among dharmas."

28. Not Receiving and Not Wanting to Receive

"Subhuti, if one bodhisattva gives away enough precious jewels to fill as many worlds as there are grains of sand in the Ganges River, and if a second knows that all dharmas are without self and thus attains patience, then the goodness attained by the second bodhisattva is superior to the first bodhisattva. Subhuti, this is because all bodhisattvas do not receive goodness."

Subhuti said to the Buddha, "World-honored One, why do you say that bodhisattvas do not receive goodness?"

"Subhuti, bodhisattvas should not be greedy or attached to the goodness that they do; this is why I say that they do not receive goodness."

29. Awesome Tranquility

"Subhuti, if someone says, 'It seems as if the Tathagata comes and goes, and sits and lies down,' then this person has not understood my meaning. And why is this? The one who is the Tathagata has not come from somewhere, and he is not going somewhere, and that is why he is called the Tathagata."

30. Compound Lakshana

"Subhuti, if a good man or a good woman were to pulverize a great chiliocosm into fine dust, what do you say, would that collection of fine dust be a lot or not?"

"It would be a lot, World-honored One. And why is this? If that collection of fine dust were something that really existed, the

Buddha would not have called it a collection of fine dust. And why is this? The Buddha has said that a collection of fine dust is not a collection of fine dust and so it is called a collection of fine dust. World-honored One, the great chiliocosm that the Tathagata has spoken about is not a great chiliocosm and that is what is called a great chiliocosm. And why is this? If that great chiliocosm really existed, then it would be a compound lakshana. The Tathagata has said that a compound lakshana is not a compound lakshana, and so it is called a compound lakshana."

"Subhuti, that which is a compound lakshana cannot really be spoken about, and yet ordinary people are attached to it and greedy about it."

31. Not Giving Rise to Belief in Lakshana

"Subhuti, if a person were to say, 'The Tathagata teaches a view of self, a view of human beings, a view of sentient beings, and a view of souls,' Subhuti, what do you say, has this person understood the meaning of what I am saying?"

"No, World-honored One. This person has not understood the meaning of what the Tathagata is saying. And why is this? The World-honored One has said that a view of self, a view of human beings, a view of sentient beings, and a view of souls is not a view of self, a view of human beings, a view of sentient beings, and a view of souls, and so it is called a view of self, a view of human beings, a view of sentient beings, and a view of souls."

"Subhuti, one who commits to highest complete enlightenment should not give rise to lakshana of dharmas; and he should know all dharmas in this way; he should view them like this, believe them, and understand them like this. Subhuti, the Tathagata says that that which is called a lakshana of a dharma is not a lakshana of a dharma, and so it is called a lakshana of a dharma."

32. *Like Shadows, Like Bubbles, Like Dreams*

"Subhuti, if a person performs an act of generosity by giving away as many precious jewels as would fill illimitable eons of worlds, and if a good man or a good woman commits to the bodhisattva mind and upholds as few as four verses of this sutra, upholds them, reads them, chants them, and teaches them, his or her goodness will be greater than that of the first person. And how should this sutra be taught to people? By not grasping lakshana, by remaining immobile in this consciousness. And why is this?

> *All conditioned dharmas*
> *are like dreams, like illusions,*
> *like bubbles, like shadows,*
> *like dew, like lightning,*
> *and all of them should be contemplated*
> *in this way."*

When the Buddha finished speaking this sutra, the elder Subhuti, along with all the monks, nuns, *upasaka, upasika, ashuras,* and worldly and heavenly beings, heard what the Buddha had said, and all of them were greatly pleased, and they all believed it, received it, and practiced it.

Wisdom

WISDOM PUBLICATIONS

Please fill out and return this card if you would like to receive our catalogue and special offers. The postage is already paid!

NAME

ADDRESS

CITY / STATE / ZIP / COUNTRY

EMAIL

Sign up for our newsletter and special offers at wisdompubs.org

Wisdom Publications is a non-profit charitable organization.

BUSINESS REPLY MAIL

FIRST-CLASS MAIL   PERMIT NO. 1100   SOMERVILLE, MA

POSTAGE WILL BE PAID BY ADDRESSEE

WISDOM PUBLICATIONS
199 ELM ST
SOMERVILLE MA 02144-9908

Commentary by
Master Hsing
Yun

1 The Causes of This Dharma Meeting

Thus have I heard.[1] *At one time, the Buddha was in the state of Shravasti*[2] *at the Jeta Grove*[3] *with a gathering of monks numbering 1,250. At mealtime, the World-honored One*[4] *put on his robe, picked up his bowl, and went into the city of Shravasti to beg for food. After he had gone from house to house,*[5] *he returned to the grove. When he had finished eating, he put away his robe and bowl, washed his feet, straightened his mat,*[6] *and sat down.*

All Buddhist sutras begin with a description of the six basic causes or conditions that allowed the words of the sutra to be spoken and remembered. They all start with a sentence that goes roughly like this: "Thus have I heard: at one time the Buddha was in [such and such a place] where there was a gathering of people [to whom he was going to speak]." The six basic conditions described in this one sentence are as follows:

1. *Thus.* In this single word the condition of accuracy is met.

2. *have I heard.* In these three words, the condition of having someone to hear the Buddha and report on what he heard is met.

3. *at one time.* The condition of time is met.

4. *the Buddha.* The condition of having a buddha to speak is met.

5. *at such and such a place.* The condition of place is met.

6. a *gathering of people.* The condition of having an audience is met.

If even one of these six conditions had been absent, there would have been no talk, or no record of the talk. The Buddha taught that all things are caused—because there is this, there is that. If you take away this, you will also take away that. It is important to appreciate the causes and conditions that give rise to any event that we wish to understand deeply. This is especially true for the very profound causes that give rise to a talk by a buddha. A buddha comes into the world only if there are people who are prepared to listen to him.

As we ponder the causes that lead to the Buddha giving the teachings contained in the *Diamond Sutra*, it is important that we also contemplate the profound causes that have given rise to our being exposed to them now. While those of us who are alive today may not have the good fortune of hearing Shakyamuni Buddha speak with our own ears, we do have the good fortune of discovering this sutra. If conditions are right, we will encounter the Dharma in this life and find ourselves receptive to it. If conditions are not right, it will pass us by. Though we were not part of the original audience that was present at the Jeta Grove and who heard these teachings firsthand, we are very much part of the extended audience that is privileged to learn of them now.

THE "I" OF THE PHRASE "THUS HAVE I HEARD"

The Buddha spoke so often about "selflessness" and the emptiness of the self that one might wonder why all Buddhist sutras begin with the phrase "thus have I heard." At an ordinary level, the "I" of this phrase refers to Ananda, one of the Buddha's principal disciples. When the Buddha neared the time of his passing from this world, he told

Ananda that all records of his teachings should begin with the phrase "thus have I heard." The Buddha instructed Ananda to use this phrase so that people would know that what they were about to hear was a true teaching of the Buddha, honestly remembered by one of his most intelligent disciples. The Buddha chose Ananda to be the witness to his teachings because Ananda had been by his side for many years, and because Ananda had an excellent memory.

At a deeper level, the "I" of this opening phrase is simply a sign of the truth. It is a symbol of the many conditions that came together to produce a teaching by a buddha. In the deepest sense, there is no Ananda to hear and there is no Buddha to speak; the very medium of sound itself is empty of ultimate reality, as are the sense organs that perceive sound and the vocal organs that produce it. The Buddha's instructions to begin all of his teachings with "Thus have I heard" was an act of compassion intended to lead sentient beings toward the truth. The phrase itself is not the truth, nor is the sutra the truth; they merely indicate the truth. They are like a finger pointing at the moon; it shows us where to look, but it is not itself the moon. The *Diamond Sutra* teaches us how to see beyond the delusion of self and beyond the many false things this delusion causes us to believe that we are perceiving. It teaches us that the "I," which the ego believes is preeminent, is nothing more than an empty projection caused by the conditions of the body and conventions of speech.

"AT ONE TIME" INDICATES A REALM BEYOND TIME

All Buddhist sutras begin with the phrase, "Thus have I heard. At one time..." This phrase does not indicate a specific time, but only a general notion of something occurring in time, or a general notion of many things coming together "at one time." At an ordinary level, this time marker is used to assure people that the teaching in the sutra was actually spoken by the Buddha and heard by Ananda at a specific time. At a deeper level, time itself is dependent on the karma of the people gathered to listen to the Buddha. At a level even deeper still, all buddhas are entirely beyond time.

Just as we must appreciate the profundity of the causes that produce a teaching given by a buddha, so we must also appreciate the profundity of the phrase "at one time." The enlightened consciousness of a buddha resides within truths that both transcend and suffuse all time everywhere. Time is not the same for all of us. Each one of us will have a different perception of when the Buddha spoke the teachings contained in the *Diamond Sutra*. To an ordinary person, the Buddha spoke the sutra 2,500 years ago; to an enlightened master, the Buddha is speaking the sutra right now. If our karma is right, "at one time" means now.

ULTIMATE WISDOM
IS NOTHING IF IT IS NOT LIFE ITSELF

The first section of the *Diamond Sutra* details the most ordinary of activities—the Buddha takes up his bowl, begs for food, returns to Jeta Grove, washes his feet, straightens his mat, and sits. It is essential that one understand the unity of the ordinary and the ultimate, the commonplace and the transcendental, if one wants to understand the *Diamond Sutra*. This unity is a principal teaching of the *Diamond Sutra*. Like a great artist, the Buddha not only says what he means, he also shows us what he means. Ultimate wisdom and ordinary reality are inextricably entwined. They cannot be separated; even the Buddha had to get his own food and straighten his own mat. Ultimate wisdom is life itself seen in the clearest of lights; it is not some other world. The bliss of nirvana resides in each and every thing in the universe; nothing is excepted.

Master P'u Wan says that this sutra begins with a scene from ordinary life in order to "reveal the depth of the true mind," and "to show people that the ordinary consciousness of daily life is no different from that of all buddhas."

A story from the Ch'an canon elucidates this truth in another way:

One day during the T'ang Dynasty, Master Hui Hai went to visit Master Tao Yi (709–788). Master Tao Yi said, "Why have you come to see me?"

Master Hui Hai replied, "I came in search of the Dharma."

Master Tao Yi said, "I don't have anything for you here. You already have untold treasures within you. Why do you come to me looking for something I cannot give you?"

Master Hui Hai asked, "Then please tell me about the treasures you say that I have within me. Where are they and how am I to know them?"

Master Tao Yi said, "The moment you ask me that question—in that moment—the treasures that are within you are fully revealed. In that moment, everything within you is fulfilled, and there is no reason at all for you to seek anything outside yourself."

In the *Diamond Sutra* the Buddha teaches us how to see ourselves in this light. He shows us how to awaken the entire fullness of our inner wisdom. He shows us how to understand that the bliss of nirvana lies in each and every thing in the universe, and that it does not lie somewhere else.

2 Subhuti's Request

At that time the elder monk Subhuti [7] was among the gathering of monks. He rose from his seat, bared his right shoulder, [8] kneeled on his right knee, and with palms pressed together before him, respectfully spoke to the Buddha saying, "Rare One, World-honored One, the Tathagata [9] protects and is concerned about all bodhisattvas, [10] and he instructs all bodhisattvas. World-honored One, when good men and good women commit themselves [11] to highest complete enlightenment, [12] on what should they base themselves, [13] and how should they subdue their minds?" [14]

The Buddha said, "Wonderful! Wonderful! Subhuti, you said that the Tathagata protects and is concerned about all bodhisattvas, and that he instructs all bodhisattvas. Now listen carefully while I tell you, when good men and good women commit themselves to highest complete enlightenment, on what they should base themselves, and how they should subdue their minds."

"Excellent, World-honored One. I eagerly await your answer."

In this section Subhuti stands and asks the Buddha to speak about prajna. Two questions may arise at this point. One of them is why did someone need to ask the Buddha to speak, why didn't he just begin his talk without being asked? The other one is why are all of the other monks quiet, why does only Subhuhti rise to ask the Buddha to talk about prajna?

There are two basic reasons why the Buddha waited to be asked about this subject before speaking on it. The first is he wanted to emphasize the value of the teaching and inspire in his listeners a strong desire to learn. The second reason lies in the person of Subhuti. Subhuti had a reputation for understanding emptiness better than any of the Buddha's other disciples. Indeed, the Buddha often asked Subhuti to explain emptiness to others. Thus, his rising to ask the Buddha about this subject is an indication of the profundity and completeness of the teaching that is about to follow. His seniority on the subject of emptiness is also the reason why he alone represented all of the other monks.

The great Chinese master Tao An (312–385 C.E.) said that all Buddhist sutras can be divided into three basic parts: an introduction to the teaching, the teaching, and a conclusion to the teaching. Section one was the introduction to this sutra. The two questions asked by Subhuti in this section begin the actual teaching of the *Diamond Sutra*. Simply stated, Subhuti asks the Buddha on what a person should base his mind and how he should control his mind. In asking the Buddha on what a person should base his mind, Subhuti is asking the Buddha about the foundation of consciousness. Since the foundation of consciousness is itself conscious, the Buddha's answer can sometimes be hard to follow. Most of us are quite adept at thinking about things either outside ourselves or inside ourselves, as if the two were split apart. We are good at subject-object relationships, but less comfortable contemplating the awareness that underlies both our thinking and our "selves." The *Diamond Sutra* will show us how to get past these difficulties and understand the very foundation of awareness.

When Subhuti asks the Buddha how a person should "subdue his mind," he is asking the Buddha how to control defiled thoughts and tendencies; that is, thoughts and tendencies born of greed, anger, or ignorance. It is one of the Buddha's teachings that once the defiled tendencies of the mind are completely eliminated, the mind will be in a state of enlightenment.

In a manner of speaking, all of the teachings of the Buddha are concerned with nothing but these two questions: On what should we base our minds, and how should we subdue their defiled tendencies? In this section, Subhuti poses these important questions. In the sections that follow, the Buddha presents what is perhaps his single greatest answer to them. Though the precision and directness of his answer can sometimes make the *Diamond Sutra* difficult to understand, at other times that same directness will leap into our minds with a brilliance we would never have imagined beforehand. To understand this sutra, we must flow with it and allow it to work its magic on us. Reading it can be like splashing spring water on your face; for an instant the water is right there, so close to you and in perfect conformity to your features, and then it is gone. The foundation of consciousness must be glimpsed many times before it can be clearly comprehended.

COMMITTING TO
HIGHEST COMPLETE ENLIGHTENMENT

Subhuti's question is based on the vow or the commitment of "good men and good women" to attain highest complete enlightenment. Highest complete enlightenment is a translation of the Sanskrit term, *anuttara-samyak-sambodhi*. To commit oneself to it is to commit oneself to becoming a buddha, an enlightened one. The term *anuttara-samyak-sambodhi* occurs twenty-nine times in the *Diamond Sutra*.

The *Mahaprajnaparamita Sutra* says, "When we shoot an arrow at a target, sometimes we hit it and sometimes we miss it. When we shoot an arrow at the ground, however, we never miss. Committing ourselves to becoming a buddha is like shooting an arrow at the ground. There is no one who cannot do it."

The concept of intention is central to the teachings of the Buddha. A vow or a commitment is one of the purest forms of intention. Buddhists sometimes compare a vow or a commitment to a magic pearl that has the power to make a pool of dirty water crystal clear simply by being placed in it. In this metaphor, the pool of dirty water stands for a defiled mind, while the clear water stands for the enlightened mind in which all defiled tendencies have been subdued. The magic pearl of commitment is the single greatest means we have to subdue our defiled thoughts and tendencies. We will have occasion to speak more about intention and commitment as we go along. For now, it is sufficient to remark that the deepest and most important quality of human consciousness is intention. Our minds, our worlds, and our relationships with all things are wholly dependent on the intentions we have toward them.

Master Chi Tsang (549–623) said, "Sentient beings suffer from two kinds of diseases: one is diseases of the body—sickness, old age, and death; and the other is diseases of the mind—greed, anger, and ignorance. Without prajna, no one has ever succeeded in curing these diseases. The Buddha taught the *Diamond Sutra* to cure these two kinds of disease."

3 The Heart of the Mahayana

PART I

The Buddha said to Subhuti, "All great bodhisattvas[15] should subdue

their minds in the following manner: they should realize as they vow

to save all sentient beings[16] that in truth there are no sentient beings

to be saved.[17] And they should realize as they vow to save all of the

infinite, innumerable, illimitable sentient beings that in reality there

are no sentient beings to be saved. When they vow to lead them all to

nirvana[18] without remainder—be they born of eggs, wombs,

moisture, or transformation, or whether they have form, or no form,

or whether they are able to perceive, or do not perceive, or cannot

perceive, or will not perceive[19]—they should realize that in truth

there are no sentient beings to be led to nirvana."

A lot of unnecessary difficulty can creep into our attempt to understand this sutra if we allow ourselves to become lost in details. The kinds of beings described by the Buddha and the kinds of logical statements he uses sometimes cause people to become confused about the much more important meaning of this passage as a whole. The Buddha uses logical terms and categories of being that were part of the philosophical landscape of ancient India. It is very profitable and interesting to think about those categories and terms, but we should not allow ourselves to become confused by them. The categories of being that are mentioned in this section are mentioned only to show that the Buddha means all sentient beings without exception. Whether they have form or no form, no matter how they are produced, no matter how they perceive, no matter what they perceive, or even if they perceive, all of them, says the Buddha, are without an absolute self-nature.

THE BODHISATTVA VOW

The bodhisattva vow is the defining feature of Mahayana Buddhism. The vow, which can be taken by anyone at any time, commits the practitioner to a life of compassion. The most common form of the bodhisattva vow practiced in China comes from the *Platform Sutra of the Sixth Patriarch*. It has four parts:

1. The vow to save all sentient beings no matter how many there are.
2. The vow to end all forms of delusion no matter how many there are.
3. The vow to learn all methods for doing the above no matter how long it takes.
4. The vow to achieve perfect enlightenment within the Buddha-dharma no matter how long it takes.

In this section of the *Diamond Sutra*, the Buddha discusses this vow. It is important to understand that his discussion is relevant to all of us, not just to bodhisattvas, for in this section the Buddha begins his discourse on the essence of consciousness.

Ch'an Master Hung Jen (602–675) said, "If you are unwilling to understand yourself, it is useless to study the Dharma. To know your own mind and your own nature is to be a buddha."

The Buddha begins his discussion with the bodhisattva vow because it is central to his wisdom teachings and is ultimately fundamental to all forms of consciousness; profound awareness is compassionate awareness. In this section, the Buddha begins to define what a sentient being really is, what a bodhisattva really is, and what it really means to be enlightened.

THERE ARE NO SENTIENT BEINGS TO BE SAVED

Sentient beings are beings with awareness, or the potential to become aware. When the Buddha says, "there are no sentient beings to be saved," he is saying that no sentient being has a permanent or absolute "self-nature." They are beings and they are aware, but there is nothing permanent about them. Buddhists call this absence of a permanent self-nature "emptiness." "Emptiness" is the usual English translation of the Sanskrit word *shunyata,* which means "devoid of an essence" or "devoid of an absolute self-nature." Emptiness does not mean that sentient beings do not exist; it only means that they have no unchanging, absolute, or permanent existence.

Emptiness applies not just to sentient beings, but also to phenomena. Phenomena are also empty. Not one of them has anything permanent or absolute about it. Everything within the phenomenal universe is empty. The Buddha taught that there is nothing that you can think about that is not empty. The concept of emptiness is very important in Buddhism, and it is crucial to the *Diamond Sutra.* To understand this sutra, one must understand the concept of emptiness. "Emptiness" does not mean that things do not exist. It only means that they have no permanent aspect whatsoever. We will discuss emptiness in more detail later. For now, we will confine our discussion to the idea that all sentient beings are empty, and therefore "there are no sentient beings to be saved."

The *Mahaprajnaparamita Sutra* says, "The essence of all sentient beings is emptiness; there is nothing in them to be emptied out of them. They already are buddhas; their buddha nature does not need to be established."

The *Awakening of Faith in the Mahayana* says, "Know that all sentient beings are the same as you and that in essence they do not differ at all from Buddha."

In this section of the *Diamond Sutra,* the Buddha says, "While saving the infinite, illimitable, innumerable sentient beings, realize that in reality there are no sentient beings to be saved."

No sentient being has a permanent or absolute self. There are no absolute coordinates that can define selfhood or individuality. Our notions of having separate selves are delusions that spring from misunderstanding who we really are. To say that the notion of individuality is based on delusion is not to say that there is no such thing as awareness. Ultimately the delusive awareness that believes it is an individual self will come to understand that it is not an individual, but part of a much greater whole; ultimately it will understand that it is a buddha.

The Buddha taught that sentient beings suffer because they do not realize that their "selves" are empty. A bodhisattva seeks to save them by helping them realize that, while they do not have an absolute self-nature, they do have a buddha nature. Their buddha nature rests in nirvana. Sentient beings attain nirvana when they free themselves from the delusions of having a separate self. The apparent contradiction between not having a self and saving other selves is one of the most important themes of the *Diamond Sutra.*

It is very significant that this sutra begins with a discussion of the vow "to save all sentient beings" because this vow emphasizes that enlightenment is not a static state. Enlightenment without compassion is not enlightenment; wisdom that is not concerned about the beings in this world is not true wisdom. Ultimate truths that are not practiced within the realm of phenomena are not ultimate truths; they are, at best, imitations of ultimate truths and nothing more.

NIRVANA

One of the Buddha's most fundamental teachings is the teaching of the three Dharma seals. The three Dharma seals are impermanence, emptiness, and nirvana. The Buddha said that all things in the phenomenal universe are "stamped" with each of the three Dharma seals; there is nothing anywhere in the universe that does not possess all three of these qualities. In the section above we briefly discussed the second Dharma seal—emptiness. In this section, we will discuss nirvana. In later sections, we will discuss impermanence.

The Buddha said that life is full of suffering, but he also said that once the causes of suffering are fully understood, one can attain nirvana. *Nirvana* is a Sanskrit word that means "extinguished" or "gone out" in the sense that a candle flame can be extinguished or go out. When one attains nirvana, all suffering is extinguished. Master P'u Wan says that there are four basic kinds of nirvana.

1. The basic nirvana inherent in all sentient beings. The basic nature of all sentient beings is pure, undefiled buddha nature. At this level there is no difference between a Buddha and an ordinary sentient being.
2. The nirvana of an enlightened person who still possesses a body. Such a person has realized the truth, but since he possesses a body, he still must endure physical trials such as heat, cold, old age, sickness, and death.
3. The nirvana of an enlightened person who does not fully understand the importance of compassion. Such a person comprehends the essence of consciousness, but he still does not comprehend the use of it.
4. The nirvana of buddhas and bodhisattvas. The highest form of nirvana occurs when profound awareness of the essence of consciousness is coupled with an equally profound understanding of the importance of compassionate intent. This nirvana is called "unattached nirvana" or the "nirvana in which they do not reside" (Sanskrit: *apratishtita nirvana*). It is given these names because the beings who attain it do not remain in nirvana. Instead, they draw on their achievement to help others realize the same thing.

Nirvana means the complete extinguishing of all defiled tendencies; the emptying out of the mind of all greed, anger, and ignorance. Nirvana is not a negative state. To be in nirvana is to completely understand both the essence and the immensity of consciousness. When the dust clears from the sky, the sky is still there. One of the deepest ideas of the *Diamond Sutra* is that nirvana is always everywhere and that it can never be separated from the here and now.

3 The Heart of the Mahayana (continued)

PART 2

"And why is this? Subhuti, if a bodhisattva has lakshana[20] of self,

lakshana of human beings, lakshana of sentient beings, or lakshana

of a soul,[21] then he is not a bodhisattva."[22]

The most commonly used word in the Diamond Sutra is *lakshana* (Chinese: *hsiang*). It is important to understand what is meant by this word if one wants to understand this sutra. *Lakshana* is often translated in English as "mark," "sign," or "characteristic." Since these English words have their own histories and associations, using them can lead to many misunderstandings. In this translation, we will simply use the word lakshana.

The word lakshana occurs eighty-four times in the *Diamond Sutra*. It is always associated with an act of perception, cognition, or thought. One of the principal teachings of this sutra is that all of our "normal" thoughts and perceptions are composed of nothing more than delusive lakshana. In this sutra, the Buddha shows us how this is so, why this is so, and what to do about it.

Generally speaking, the word lakshana in Buddhism refers to deluded awareness. Lakshana might be thought of as the building blocks of delusion; they can be thoughts, perceptions, memories, dreams, emotions, or any other element of awareness. Deluded lakshana arise, abide, and disappear. Though they have no self-nature, they are exceptionally entrancing, and so we cling to them and bring suffering to ourselves.

The *Lankavatara Sutra* says, "All of the many different shapes, aspects, and forms of things are what is called lakshana."

Ultimately, all lakshana are manifestations of karma. The *Treatise on the Perfection of Great Wisdom* says that there are two basic kinds of lakshana—general lakshana, and particular lakshana. Impermanence is an example of a general lakshana since all things are impermanent, while the shape of an object is an example of a particular lakshana since that shape does not occur everywhere.

The *Abhidharmamahavibhasa Shastra* says that all conditioned phenomena possess four basic lakshana: a lakshana of arising, a lakshana of abiding, a lakshana of changing, and a lakshana of extinction.

The *Commentary on the Ten Stages Sutra* says that all things possess six basic lakshana: general lakshana, particular lakshana, the lakshana of sameness, the lakshana of difference, the lakshana of growth, and the lakshana of decline.

Master Ching K'ung said, "In a word, buddha nature is real and true, while all lakshana are delusions. To become enlightened means to return to buddha nature by ceasing to cling to lakshana."

The *Vijnaptimatratasiddhi Shastra* says, "Being attached to lakshana means that one does not understand that the lakshana of one's realm are delusions…and thus one cannot find peace."

Lakshana can be anything that we perceive or know. The *Maharatnakuta* says, "The basic nature of all dharmas is emptiness; the self-nature of all dharmas is no-nature. If all things are empty and without self-nature, then each and every lakshana is no-lakshana (Sanskrit: *alakshana*). Purity is attained through no-lakshana. If all things are empty and without self nature, then they cannot be revealed by lakshana."

The Northern version of the *Parinirvana Sutra* says that nirvana can be called "no-lakshana." The sutra says that nirvana is "without lakshana of form, lakshana of sound, lakshana of smell, lakshana of taste, lakshana of touch, lakshana of rising, lakshana of abiding, lakshana of declining, lakshana of male, or lakshana of female."

The *Glossary of Esoteric Terms* says that the term "no-lakshana" has a shallow and a deep meaning. The shallow meaning is that each and every dharma is empty, devoid of self-nature, and without absolute shape or form. The deep meaning is that although each and every dharma in the universe contains all other dharmas in the universe, still no single, absolute dharma can ever be found anywhere.

Buddhist masters also speak of teaching with lakshana and teaching without lakshana, of practicing with lakshana and practicing without lakshana, of contemplating lakshana and contemplating no-lakshana, and of realms with lakshana and realms without lakshana.

Though lakshana usually refer to deluded awareness, they do not always do so, for a buddha is able to see them and know them. From the human point of view, lakshana are the stuff of deluded awareness; from a buddha's point of view, they are nothing more than "illusions, shadows, bubbles, dew."

Though lakshana are subjective delusions that are made and held in the mind, they are almost always treated as if they were objectively real. The *Mahaparinirvana Sutra* makes it clear that there is nothing absolute or permanent about them at all. The sutra says, "If anyone were to believe that dharmas have either universal or particular lakshana that are absolute, then you should know that that person will create a lakshana of form upon seeing a form, a lakshana of knowledge upon seeing something known, a lakshana of a man upon seeing a man, a lakshana of a woman upon seeing a woman, a lakshana of the sun upon seeing the sun, a lakshana of the moon upon seeing the moon, a lakshana of a time upon sensing time, a lakshana of the five *skandhas* upon seeing the five skandhas, a lakshana of the senses upon experiencing the senses, and a lakshana of a realm upon seeing a realm. And when such a person sees like this, he or she fastens himself to a demon, and becomes a demon. Such a person's mind is not pure."

This brief discussion should give some idea of how the word lakshana generally is used in Buddhism. In the *Diamond Sutra*, the Buddha uses this word to bore to the heart of human awareness. Lakshana is the single most important word in the *Diamond Sutra*. The Buddha's repeated use of this word, and his consistent denial that it denotes anything but delusion, shows clearly that the people of his time and place had the same tendencies as people have today; then, as now, people tended to cling to lakshana as if they were solid and immutable entities that could provide comfort and security to the mind. In some of his discourses, the Buddha teaches that life is full of suffering because everything is impermanent; in others, he teaches that nothing has an absolute self-nature or essence. In the *Diamond Sutra*, he teaches us how to understand the fundamental delusion of selfhood, the delusion of believing that we really are individual people, or individual sentient beings, or individual souls, or that anybody else is.

In this section the Buddha says, "If a bodhisattva has lakshana of self, lakshana of human beings, lakshana of sentient beings, or lakshana of a soul, then he is not a bodhisattva." This means that any and all notions of individuality are delusions. No notion of selfhood is real. All lakshana of self are false. To make this point as forcefully as he can, the Buddha states that all notions related to the delusion of selfhood are false; not only is the self a delusion, but so too is the notion of a human being, a sentient being, or a soul. If a bodhisattva believes that any of these constructs are real—i.e., has a lakshana of any of them—then such a one is not a bodhisattva.

Some commentators say that this statement is the theme of the entire sutra, that everything that follows is nothing more than an explanation of this statement. While there is some truth to this claim, we should not believe that this is the only teaching in the *Diamond Sutra*. The themes of compassion and generosity are also central to this sutra.

SOUL

The word *soul* (Chinese: *shou che*) in the above quotation might also be interpreted as meaning an "entity that lives for a long time," an "entity that perdures over time," or an "entity that reincarnates." Master Tao Yuan (1911–88) said that *shou che* means that part of us that "clings to life." Chiang Wei-nung (1873–1938) said *shou che* means, "continu-

ous clinging to the lakshana of self, human being, or sentient being."
Huang Nien-tzu said, "*Shou che* is that which is continually passed
along in the *alaya* consciousness." Reasonable arguments can be made
for any one of these interpretations. The significant point, however, is
that this word is one part of the Buddha's categorical denial of selfhood.
All lakshana of self, no matter how we conceive of them, are false. All
of them lead to deeper entanglements with delusion.

Master Ching K'ung said, "The four lakshana [self, human being,
sentient being, soul] mean nothing more than 'lakshana of self.'"

Chiang Wei-nung said, "The four lakshana arise from attachment to
the lakshana of self."

Sun Chien-feng said, "The four lakshana all arise from clinging
to self."

The Buddha taught that there is no entity, no soul, and no self
that reincarnates. Only our karma is reborn. Any notion of selfhood
is a lakshana of delusion. In all of his teachings, the Buddha is always
showing us how to overcome delusion. When he claims that the
world is a delusion, he is not saying that it is not here, or that some
dreamer is dreaming it. He is saying that if you believe that this world
has absolute entities like selves, or people, or souls in it, then you are
deluded. You have not understood the depths of your own awareness. You are trapping yourself in a belief system that will inevita-
bly lead to pain. The Buddha said many times that the freedom that
results from overcoming this delusion is awesome. He spent his life
teaching us how to see this truth.

4 The Wonder of Behaving Without Attachment

"Moreover, Subhuti, within this phenomenal world,[23] *a bodhisattva ought to practice generosity*[24] *without basing it on anything.*[25] *This means that he should not base his generosity on form, and he should not base his generosity on sound, smell, taste, touch, or thought.*[26] *Subhuti, the generosity of a bodhisattva should be like this, and should not be based on any lakshana*[27] *whatsoever. And why is this? If the generosity of a bodhisattva is not based on any lakshana whatsoever, then his goodness*[28] *will be immeasurable.*

"Subhuti, what do you say, can the vastness of space to the east of us be measured?"

"No, it cannot, World-honored One."

"Subhuti, can the vastness of space in any direction[29] *be measured? Can the vastness of space to the south, west, north, up, or down be measured?"*

"No, it cannot, World-honored One."

"Subhuti, when the generosity of a bodhisattva is not based on

lakshana, his goodness is just as immeasurable as that. Subhuti,

a bodhisattva should base himself on this teaching and this

teaching alone."[30]

When Subhuti posed his first question to the Buddha he asked, "World-honored One, when good men and good women commit themselves to highest complete enlightenment, on what should they base themselves, and how should they subdue their minds?" The word *base* in this sentence can be translated many ways. The word in Chinese is *chu*, which means "to dwell, to abide, to stop, or to cease," in addition to its meaning here—"to base." Subhuti is asking the Buddha for some kind of rule or standard for his thoughts; he is asking the Buddha if there is a secure dwelling place for his mind. His question prompts the Buddha to elucidate for him the very basis of consciousness itself; Subhuti's question prompts the Buddha to give the teaching contained in the *Diamond Sutra.*

In this section the Buddha tells Subhuti that a bodhisattva must learn to act without basing his or her mind on anything at all. The bodhisattva must learn to be and to act wholly without mental attachments of any kind. This is one of the principal themes of the *Diamond Sutra.* In subsequent sections of the sutra, the Buddha will explain why this is so and how to do it. In this section, he begins to frame his argument in terms of the paramita of generosity.

The six paramitas are the basic virtues of a bodhisattva; they are also a sort of summation of all of the teachings of the Buddha, since they are the perfect unification of thought and behavior. The six paramitas are generosity, restraint, patience, diligence, concentration, and wisdom. Since human beings cannot remain still forever, they must behave in some way. The six paramitas are the highest form of human behavior. The *Diamond Sutra* is principally concerned with the paramita of wisdom; secondarily, it is concerned with the paramitas of generosity and patience. The Buddha discusses the paramitas of generosity and patience in this sutra because they are important in and of themselves and because they are perfect examples for how the paramita of wisdom should be understood. Most of the Buddha's examples in this sutra employ the paramita of generosity. Many commentators on the *Diamond Sutra* have pointed out that for the sake of brevity, the Buddha used generosity to represent all the paramitas.

Chiang Wei-nung said, "The ancients all explained this section by saying that generosity stands for all six of the paramitas as well as all other forms of practice. That is why the Buddha spoke only about generosity."

There are several important kinds of generosity recognized in Buddhism. The first, and most obvious, is material generosity. When we give something of value to someone we are engaging in material generosity. The second is helping people to let go of fear. The Buddha taught that fearlessness can be a gift. We give this gift whenever we behave with compassion, kindness, patience, or moral propriety. The third form of generosity is the most important; this is the gift of the Dharma. Whenever we teach the Dharma, disseminate Dharma literature, or discuss the Dharma with others, we are giving the highest of all gifts, because only the Dharma has the power to help others understand the truth. Material gifts bring comfort to others; the gift of fearlessness frees their spirits; and the gift of the Dharma shows them how to overcome all suffering.

There are many reasons why the Buddha used generosity in his discussion of non-attachment. First among these is the simple importance of generosity; it is basic to our relations with others. Second among these is that the Buddha did not want anyone to come to the mistaken conclusion that being non-attached means being inactive or not caring about others.

Thirdly, the Buddha chose the subject of generosity to begin his inquiry into the foundation of consciousness because it is more or less obvious that generosity with strings attached is not real generosity. When gift-givers have ulterior motives, their gifts bring none of the pleasant states described above, but only suspicion and mistrust. We all know what it is like to be on the receiving end of such "generosity." In this section, the Buddha asks us to understand why we can and should give freely, without expecting anything in return. While we may often pretend to do this, most of us rarely, if ever, give anything without expecting something in return. This seems almost impossible to do. To get around this problem, we sometimes speak of "higher selfishness" or "spiritual selfishness." The Buddha is asking us to go higher still and discover in ourselves "generous selflessness." The level of generosity he describes in this section is so deep and so central to the foundation of our consciousness that it mingles philosophy with morality. In Buddhism, philosophy is morality, and morality is philosophy. How could the truth of conscious existence ever be otherwise?

Ch'an Master Lin Chi (?–867) often spoke of the "true person without station," that deep part of us that is more fundamental than social distinctions, class, background, language, or thought. Although this part of us is obvious, most of us cannot find it, because we use thought and language to look for it. When Ch'an Master Hui K'o (487–593) begged Bodhidharma (?–535) to pacify his (Hui Ko's) mind, Bodhidharma replied, "Give me your mind." The elusive nature of mind is the subject of hundreds of Ch'an stories because by teasing us into thinking about our minds, Ch'an masters also teach us that the mind has no absolute foundation; the more we look for it, the less we are able to find it. For this reason, the Buddha tells us in this section that "if the generosity of a bodhisattva is not based on lakshana, his goodness will be...immeasurable." If we base an act of generosity on lakshana, we prevent that act from springing from the depths of our true mind, and thus we prevent ourselves from knowing our mind as it really is.

One day Ch'an Master Chao Chou (778–897) saw his disciple, Wen Yuan, prostrating himself before an image of the Buddha. Master Chao Chou struck Wen Yuan with a stick and said, "What the hell are you doing?"

Confused, Wen Yuan replied, "I am bowing to the Buddha; I have done nothing wrong!"

Master Chao Chou said, "What the hell are you doing that for?"

Wen Yuan said, "It's a good thing to bow to the Buddha…"

Master Chao Chou lifted his stick and struck Wen Yuan again saying, "A good thing is never as good as no thing!"

This section of the *Diamond Sutra* is like a stick across our backs. It is meant to break apart our entrancements with our own goodness and generosity. It teaches us not to cling to generous deeds in any way, for in clinging to them, we ruin them and falsify ourselves. The generosity described in this section also provides us with a comparatively "easy" example of human thought and behavior that is not based on lakshana. If we can understand what the Buddha means by selfless generosity, then we will be in a good position to understand the content of the rest of the *Diamond Sutra*.

5 Seeing the Truth That Lies Beneath Perception

"Subhuti, what do you say, can you see the Tathagata in his

bodily lakshana?"[31]

"No, World-honored One, no one can see the Tathagata in

his bodily lakshana. And why is this? The bodily lakshana that

the Tathagata is talking about are not bodily lakshana."

The Buddha said to Subhuti, "All lakshana are delusive. If

you can see that all lakshana are not lakshana,[32] *then you will*

see the Tathagata."

In this section, the Buddha moves his argument forward. Building on the insight that generosity can be good only when it is true, and that true generosity must not be attached to any phenomenal form or reward, he informs Subhuti that everything is like this. Truth cannot be found by clinging to anything within the phenomenal world; the foundation of consciousness is deeper than any phenomenal perception. Just as a bodhisattva must learn to "base" his generosity on the non-base of complete non-attachment, so he must learn to base his consciousness on the non-base of complete non-attachment to any phenomenon whatsoever.

The brilliance of the Buddha can be seen not only in what he says, but also in the way in which he crafts his explanations. Ch'an Master Hui Neng (638–713) said, "Generosity should be practiced with a pure and undefiled mind. One should not be generous because one wants to look good, or because one hopes to gratify some desire through one's actions. True generosity inwardly teaches us to overcome egotism as outwardly we help others." When we are truly generous without expecting anything in return, we achieve a profound state of wisdom. The consciousness of someone who is generous without attachment is triumphant; it has achieved, however briefly, perfect moral and philosophical liberation. The awareness of someone who is generous without basing his generosity on any phenomenal perception whatsoever is liberated awareness; that state of awareness, however briefly it lasts, is enlightenment. It is a direct glimpse into the mind of a buddha. In an act of perfect generosity, there is no awareness of a giver, a gift, or a recipient of a gift. There is nothing but the undefiled goodness of the enlightened mind.

Surely all of us have glimpsed this state. In this section of the *Diamond Sutra,* the Buddha helps us use this glimpse to begin to see that all of our perceptions and all of our attachments should be understood in this same way. When we base our minds on our attachments, we suffer; when we base them on pure and undefiled consciousness, we triumph.

THE TATHAGATA

One of the ten principal names of the Buddha is Tathagata. *Tathagata* means "thus-come one" in English. *Thusness* means the complete nowness and "thisness" of the here and now. It is awareness without filters, without distance, without mediating concepts. It is awareness in the raw, perfect and complete, without desire for gain, without attachment to anything. Thusness is a philosophical word, but it denotes the intuitive and inviolable immediacy of poetry or love. The Tathagata, the "thus-come one," is just that, all the time and everywhere. This is the reason why it is hard to say who the Buddha is or what enlightenment really means. The thusness of the Buddha cannot be described; it can only be hinted at. No one can realize it for you.

In this section, *Tathagata* is used in two ways: (1) as a title of address, and (2) as a synonym for ultimate truth, or buddha mind. When the Buddha asks Subhuti "Can you see the Tathagata in his bodily lakshana?" he is asking about ultimate truth. When Subhuti refers to the "lakshana that the Tathagata is talking about," he is simply addressing the Buddha. To appreciate the profundity of the *Diamond Sutra*, we must be willing to shift our minds from one meaning to the other, for if we cling to a single interpretation we will be like one who tries to see the enlightened Buddha with his mere senses. The Buddha that Subhuti is addressing is a person, but he is also the enlightened Buddha, the Tathagata, and in this, he is infinitely greater than the mere bodily lakshana that Subhuti addresses.

ALL LAKSHANA ARE NOT LAKSHANA

All lakshana are not lakshana because they are all empty. "All lakshana are not lakshana" means that lakshana are not what they seem. While they may seem to have unchanging self-natures, they do not. If you can truly see this, you will see the Tathagata. The full explanation of why this is so is completed in the remainder of the sutra. In this section, the Buddha is making a leading assertion. He led us toward this assertion by using the example of generosity without attachment; now he leads us on a little further by giving us another "easy" example of delusive lakshana—those pertaining to the Tathagata himself. In later passages, he will say, "there are no definite dharmas." Master Chih Yi (538–597) said that the heart of the *Diamond Sutra* lies in the one line: "If you can see that all lakshana are not lakshana, then you will see the Tathagata." In this section of the *Diamond Sutra*, the Buddha directs our minds toward the next key to understanding the very essence of consciousness itself.

6 The Rarity of True Belief

Subhuti said to the Buddha, "World-honored One, can sentient

beings, upon hearing these words, really be expected to believe them?"

The Buddha told Subhuti, "Don't talk like that. Even after I[33]

have been gone for five hundred years, there will still be people who

are moral and who cultivate goodness. If they can believe this teaching

and accept it as the truth, you can be sure that they will have planted

good roots not just with one buddha, or two buddhas, or three, or

four, or five buddhas, but that they will have planted good roots with

tens of millions of buddhas. And if someone has so much as a single

pure moment of belief[34] *concerning this teaching, Subhuti, they will*

be intimately[35] *known and seen by the Tathagata. And what is the*

reason that these sentient beings will attain such infinite goodness?[36]

These sentient beings will not return to the lakshana of self, the lak-

shana of human beings, the lakshana of sentient beings, the lakshana

of souls, the lakshana of laws, or the lakshana of non-laws.

"And why is this? If a sentient being clings to lakshana in his mind,

then he will cling to self, human beings, sentient beings, or souls. If he

clings to the lakshana of a law, then he will also cling to self, human

beings, sentient beings, or souls. And why is this? If he clings to even

so little as[37] the lakshana of a non-law,[38] then he will also cling to self,

human beings, sentient beings, or souls. Thus, he must not cling to

laws or non-laws, and this is why I have often said to you monks that

even my teachings should be understood to be like a raft; if even the

Dharma must be let go of, then how much more must everything else

be let go of?"

In this section, Subhuti asks the Buddha a very simple and honest question—can anybody really be expected to believe this? With his answer to this question, the Buddha deepens his explanation of the foundation of consciousness.

In section three, the Buddha questioned the reality of individuality. In section four, he showed us how to understand this by explaining the true meaning of generosity. In section five, he deepened our understanding of truth by prompting Subhuti to declare that "no one can perceive the Tathagata in his bodily lakshana" because "all lakshana are delusive." In this section, he moves his argument forward again by pointing out that not only are all lakshana so delusive that we must not cling to them, but so are all thoughts, concepts, mental laws, and formulas.

After answering Subhuti's question, the Buddha begins teaching us that there is nothing anywhere that we can cling to, for to be attached to anything is to base our minds on delusion. Remember that, as a subtext, the Buddha is still answering Subhuti's initial question, "On what should good men and women base themselves?"

A good part of the complexity of the *Diamond Sutra* lies in the intricacy and economy of the Buddha's answers. Here he uses Subhuti's question about belief to show us that just as our understanding of generosity must be deepened, so too must our understanding of belief. Just as generosity has a very high form that partakes of the enlightened buddha mind, so too does belief have more than one simple level. The Buddha assures us that anyone who believes the teaching of the *Diamond Sutra* for a single moment will be seen and known by the Tathagata. The Tathagata is enlightened consciousness. When we look toward it, it looks toward us; belief in these teachings is an intimation of enlightenment. Just as in true generosity there is no giver, no gift, and no recipient of any gift, so in deep belief, there is no self, no Buddha, and nothing to believe. Enlightenment is perfect awareness; in belief, the self begins its journey toward perfect awareness; through intuition it begins to grade into perfect awareness. Infinite consciousness is bound by nothing since it permeates everything; in belief the self begins to see this and thus to lose itself.

More than anything else, the power of the Buddha's teaching lies in his extraordinary ability to speak about such difficult matters and to explain them so clearly. Given sufficient time to work its magic, the *Diamond Sutra* is capable of revealing to us the very foundation and source of our being. In the following sections, I shall attempt to deepen the context of the most important ideas covered in this section of the sutra.

MORALITY

The Buddha directs his answer concerning belief to those who uphold the precepts, that is, to those "who are moral." The foundation of all of the Buddha's teachings is morality; there is no other foundation. Buddhism is not a mere intellectual exercise. It is a philosophy of life, a religion of the mind, an infinitely practical teaching. The Dharma must be used to be learned. A truth that is not practiced in life and applied to life cannot be a Buddhist truth. The basis of morality is not harming other sentient beings. When we refrain from harming others, we begin to smother the roots of ignorance inside us and to extirpate the causes of delusion. Delusion is caused by defiled intentions, that is, all intentions born of greed, anger, or ignorance. Whenever anyone begins to practice harmlessness, he will begin to purify both his mind and his karma. As that process of purification proceeds, his ability to understand deep levels of truth will grow.

PLANTING GOOD ROOTS

The *Avatamsaka Sutra* says, "Belief is the mother of all virtue, and it nurtures all good roots." In the *Diamond Sutra* the Buddha says that if those "who are moral…believe this teaching…they will have planted good roots with an infinite number of buddhas."

The concept of a "root" can be quite deep in Buddhism. The roots of our phenomenal bodies are our karma. The roots of our thoughts are our intentions. The roots of our perception are the consequences of everything that we have ever done. If we have done some good, if we at least glimpse the importance of not harming others, then we must have some good roots. If you have read the *Diamond Sutra* this far, you must have many good roots. What we have and what we are depends on our various roots—our wisdom roots, our roots of generosity, our roots of patience, diligence, perseverance, compassion, and so on. These are roots that we have already planted at some time in the past. What we will become depends on the roots we are planting today. It is better to spend more time thinking about the roots that you are planting today than about the roots that you planted in the past. We can learn from the past, but we must not dwell on it. When Buddhists say "a bodhisattva fears not the result, but only the cause," they mean that we must expend the bulk of our energy planting good roots today, rather than fretting about the plants that are already growing from the roots we planted in the past.

Once a Brahmin asked the Buddha, "How should I increase my good roots?"

The Buddha replied, "To increase good roots you must be moral, study the Dharma, be generous and unattached, and you must contemplate the meaning of wisdom and emptiness."

NOT BEING ATTACHED
TO ANY MENTAL LAW OR CONCEPT OR FORMULA

Just as we bind ourselves to delusion by being attached to lakshana, so we bind ourselves to delusion when we become attached to concepts, formulas, mental patterns, or laws. There is no formula, law, or mental construct anywhere that can simply hand us the truth. We cannot just plug data into some formula and expect enlightenment. We cannot experience highest complete enlightenment by memorizing a parcel of facts. If we can see that lakshana are not the deepest level of truth, we should be able to see as well that mental constructs are not the deepest level of truth either. They may be true in a limited sense, but they can never be true in the way the Buddha means. The Buddha is teaching us how to find the very source of our awareness and to awaken within that source. If there were a formula for doing that, he would tell us so.

Ch'an Master Ch'uan said, "When floating clouds scatter, the jade blue sky is the same all around."

Hsiao Yao-weng (1562–1649) said, "When there is thought without awareness, one enters the ordinary realm. When there is thought with awareness, one enters the realm of sages. When there is no thought with awareness, one enters the saintly realm. The wise understand this, though it is hard to express in words."

THE DHARMA IS LIKE A RAFT

Not even the Dharma can be clung to. Clinging to the teachings of the Buddha would lead to error as surely as clinging to any other mental construct. The Dharma is a finger pointing at the moon; it is not the moon. It is a telescope through which we can see the moon; it is not the moon. Imagine how absurd it would be if an astronomer thought

that he could study the moon by simply looking at his telescope, and
not through it. The Dharma is a telescope, a microscope, and a tool—a
means to an end; it shows us how to find the truth, but it is not itself the
truth. At the end of this section the Buddha makes this point unequiv-
ocally by comparing the Dharma to a raft; when we have crossed the
stream, we move on, we do not carry the raft with us any more. We use
the Buddha's teachings to become wise; we do not use them to trap
ourselves in a conceptual imitation of wisdom.

In his commentary on the *Diamond Sutra*, Master P'u Wan says
that there are many ways to subdue the mind, and all of them can be
compared to rafts. He says, "Those who have not crossed the river must
use them, while those who have crossed the river must discard them."

There is a Ch'an *koan* that makes a similar point:

One cold winter it snowed for three days in a row. A beggar knocked
at Ch'an Master Jung Hsi's (1141–1215) door. Trembling with cold, the
beggar said, "My family has not eaten for days. Can you help us? We
are on the verge of starvation."

Master Jung Hsi felt great compassion for the man, but he knew that
there was no extra food in the monastery, and that he himself owned
nothing of value. Then he remembered the gold leaf that was to be used
to cover the image of the Buddha in Ch'an hall. He went to the hall
with the beggar and gave him some.

Some disciples who were in the hall said, "Master, that gold leaf is
for the Buddha. You shouldn't just give it away!"

Master Jung Hsi replied, "I am showing more respect for the Buddha
by giving it away than by keeping it."

The disciples answered, "How can that be? The gold leaf is to be used
to decorate the image of the Buddha himself!"

Master Jung Hsi replied, "All sentient beings are buddhas. The image
you refer to is just an empty sign that indicates this truth. The purpose
of the image is not to teach you to cling to it, but to teach you to cling
to nothing at all."

7 Nothing Has Been Attained and Nothing Has Been Said

"Subhuti, what do you say? Has the Tathagata really attained

highest complete enlightenment? Has the Tathagata really

spoken a Dharma?"[39]

Subhuti said, "As far as I understand what the Buddha has

said, there is no definite dharma[40] *that can be called highest*

complete enlightenment, and there is no definite Dharma[41]

that could be spoken about by the Tathagata. And why is

this? The Dharma of which the Tathagata speaks cannot be

held onto,[42] *it cannot be spoken, it is not a law, and it is not a*

non-law. And that is why all bodhisattvas understand

the unconditioned dharmas[43] *differently."*

In the last section, the Buddha said that we must not cling to anything, including his own teachings. In this section, he moves forward yet again. Having stimulated our interest in "true belief," the Buddha now smashes all belief; he has Subhuti conclude that there is no absolute state of highest complete enlightenment, and that even the Buddha himself cannot speak of anything definite. The reader might think that this is the last point that the Buddha is going to make; after all, where can he go from here? Nothing is definite; even the Buddha himself cannot speak of anything definite or absolute. Where could one go from here? These seem to be truths with no further implications. To some they may even seem to be depressing truths. Once again, the Buddha will show his mastery, for he will establish an even deeper truth on this one. But let us not rush ahead too quickly.

The *Shurangama Sutra* says, "All space in all directions resides within the mind of the Tathagata like a cloud that dots the sky." The Tathagata moves like wind through the woods; like sun and rain, he touches everything. Once when he was teaching, the Buddha lifted a few leaves with his hand. He held them up and said, "The words that I speak are like these few leaves, while the truths that I speak about are like all of the leaves in the forest."

In this section the Buddha tells us that "there is nothing to attain." He says this to clear away any last remnants of the belief that nirvana is some "place" that we go to, that enlightenment is some state that exists in some other world than this one. Remember that this sutra opened with the most ordinary of scenes; the Buddha put on his robe, went into town, begged for food, returned to the Jeta Grove, ate, washed his feet, straightened his mat, and sat down.

The *Avatamsaka Sutra* says, "If [the listeners'] roots are good, there is progress. If their roots are not good, there is sloth. He preaches the Dharma according to what they can understand."

Nothing has a self-nature, there is nothing absolute anywhere, there is nothing to attain, and nothing to say. This may seem like the end of the road, but there is one small detail that is still left standing—you are still here. The world is still here. The *Avatamsaka Sutra* says, "When the wind moves through emptiness, nothing really moves." Everything is empty, but here we are. There are no absolutes anywhere, but there go the rocks and the trees.

The *Sutra of the Precious Basket* records the following exchange:

Subhuti said, "Manjushri, what is the difference between the defiled mind and the Dharma?"

Manjushri said, "Subhuti, just as all of the light that reflects off Mount Sumeru in the evening is gold, so in the light of prajna wisdom all things are the same."

Ch'an Master Hui Neng once said, "Enlightenment is found by looking within, not by looking for mysteries outside yourself." No one can hand enlightenment to you; it is something that you must see for yourself. The *Diamond Sutra* is not mere word play. Its message is both deep and real. This teaching has the power to transform your way of looking at the world. The Buddha is not teaching us how to attain something, or gain something, or grasp something; he is teaching us how to free ourselves from the limitations of grasping and the need to attain anything at all.

Master P'u Wan makes the following comment about this section of the sutra: "If we believe that enlightenment can really be grasped or that the Dharma can really be spoken about, then we will cling to those lakshana, and fall into the error of believing in an absolute reality. Contrariwise, if we believe that there is no such thing as enlightenment and that there is no dharma that can be spoken about, then we will cling to the lakshana of no-dharma, and fall into the error of believing that there is nothing but emptiness. In either case, we will miss the insight of sages." This insight, he continues, "uses emptiness to banish belief in an absolute reality" and it "uses the immense variety of reality to banish belief in absolute emptiness."

The *Awakening of Faith in the Mahayana* says, "You must understand that defiled dharmas and pure dharmas are always intermingling with each other; neither type has so much as a single lakshana that can be defined solely in terms of itself. This is the reason why it is said that no dharma has any lakshana that can be spoken about; the deep basis of all dharmas is always without form, without mind, without wisdom, without knowledge, without being, and without nonbeing. When the Buddha spoke about these things, he was just using words to help sentient beings understand the truth. The purpose of his teachings is to help us disentangle our minds from phenomenal thoughts and return to the *bhutatathata*."

Bhutatathata is without lakshana or form. It is sometimes described as the uncreated, undifferentiated whole. Near synonyms for bhutatathata are "dharmakaya," "buddha nature," "buddha mind," and "the storehouse of the Tathagata."

The *Awakening of Faith in the Mahayana* continues the above thought in this way: "Bhutatathata is that which cannot be spoken about or thought about. If this is so, then how are sentient beings to follow these truths and enter into the bhutatathata? If you fully understand that, even though we may speak about these matters, they cannot really be spoken about, and that even though we may think about these matters, they cannot really be thought about—if you can fully understand this, then you can be said to be following these truths. If you can completely disentangle your mind from all phenomenal thought, then you can be said to have entered the bhutatathata."

Once Ch'an Master Yao Shan (751–832) was meditating outside with two of his disciples. In the near distance were two trees; one of them was dry and bare, while the other was full of leaves. Suddenly the master opened his eyes and asked one of his disciples, "Which of those two trees is better, the dry one or the one with leaves?"

His disciple replied, "The one with leaves is better."

Then Master Yao Shan asked his other disciple, "Which one do you think is better?"

The second disciple replied, "The dry one is better."

Just then a man passed by. Master Yao Shan asked him which tree he thought was better.

The man said, "The dry one has to live with its dryness, while the one with leaves has to live with its leaves, and that is all."

8 Enlightenment Comes from These Teachings

"Subhuti, what do you say? If a person, in an act of generosity, were to give away enough precious jewels [44] to fill an entire great chiliocosm,[45] would the goodness [46] he achieved be great or not?"

Subhuti said, "It would be very great, World-honored One. And why is this? This goodness is devoid of a 'goodness nature,'[47] and therefore the Tathagata would say that it is great."

"If someone else were to receive and uphold as few as four verses of this sutra, and if he were to teach them to others, his goodness would be even greater than that. And why is this? Subhuti, all buddhas and all highest complete enlightenment are born of this sutra.[48] Subhuti, that which is called the Buddhadharma is not the Buddhadharma."[49]

In this section, the Buddha emphasizes both the emptiness of his teachings on emptiness and the importance of them. This is not mere word play. The Dharma is a raft. It is essential to use the raft to cross the stream that divides understanding from non-understanding. Once the stream has been crossed, the raft must be discarded. Remember, though, that the stream being crossed in this metaphor is a stream that must be crossed again and again, and thus the raft must be used again and again. Our minds have many trains of thought and potential trains of thought; each of these trains must be led across the stream, and thus the raft of the Dharma must be used again and again. It would be a tragic mistake for anyone to believe that the teachings in the *Diamond Sutra* can be fully understood and applied after only one or two readings. The Buddha himself spent six years in intense investigation before he became enlightened; for most of us even a lifetime is not enough.

Emptiness helps us become even-minded. Even-mindedness helps us appraise our good and bad tendencies in a neutral light, and it helps us to accept the conclusions of our analyses without resistance. In this section, the Buddha emphasizes the importance of his teachings on emptiness by emphasizing the importance of the *Diamond Sutra*. Prajna wisdom is the mother of all buddhas; all good roots are nurtured by it. Once again, the "goodness" mentioned in this section is not a goodness that can be measured on any samsaric scale; this goodness partakes of the goodness of the awakened mind in much the same way that beings on earth partake of the warmth of the sun. Of course, the truly awakened mind is not at any distance from us; it is inside us. Even a small act of kindness grades into the enormous compassion and goodness of the Buddha, who is everywhere.

In this section, the Buddha compares an enormous act of material generosity to the upholding of as few as four verses of the *Diamond Sutra*. The obvious reason for his doing this is to point out that awakened wisdom is always greater than any amount of material giving. The less obvious reason is that he is again emphasizing the importance of actually doing something in the world; prajna wisdom is not a static resting place; it is a dynamic interfacing of the "self" with the self's "reality." This point is fully as important as all of the Buddha's teachings on emptiness. Indeed, one must understand this point to understand emptiness. The *Diamond Sutra* is really two texts in one; one text concerns the essence of wisdom and the foundation of consciousness, while the other text shows how that wisdom is to be understood. This is the reason that the Buddha frames his argument in terms of the bodhisattva vow. Though he tells us not to cling to acts of generosity, he never tells us not to be generous. Though he tells us not to be attached to any mental or perceptual construct, he never tells us to stop doing things altogether. This sutra is based on the assumption that the Buddha's listeners already fully understand the importance of compassionate activity; the first section of the *Diamond Sutra* could not make this point more clearly.

Many people have difficulty conjoining emptiness with compassionate activity. In large part, this sutra is nothing more than an answer to this difficulty. The Buddha's prajna teachings are not a call to go sit in a room, isolated from the world; they are a call to enter into the world in the most selfless way possible. The joy that comes from understanding these teachings is very great, for they allow the mind to free itself from its own worst enemy. In the *Diamond Sutra*, the Buddha clearly teaches that ultimate wisdom is compassionate wisdom, that the awakened mind is ineluctably one with the same compassion and goodness that characterized Shakyamuni Buddha himself. Wisdom and compassion can no more be separated from each other than the phenomenal world can be separated from emptiness, or emptiness from the phenomenal world.

PRAJNA

The deep nature of reality is emptiness. Insight into this reality is called prajna. The *Tao Te Ching* says, "The great way has no name, but we must call it something." Master Lin Chi said, "The true buddha is without form, the true way is without shape, the true Dharma is without lakshana." Prajna is a word that denotes an indescribable experience. It is one thing to know that all things are empty; it is another thing to experience that emptiness without mediating filters.

The *Samadhi Sutra* says, "When the mind has no lakshana, when it does not grasp at deluded ideas, when it does not cleave to a buddha realm, when it does not base itself on wisdom, it has [attained] the wondrous profundity of prajna paramita."

Sometimes prajna means enlightenment; at other times it means the state of wisdom that leads directly to enlightenment. In its initial stages, prajna is a powerful intuition of higher truth; it manifests as faith and a desire to become good. The six paramitas are both a description of prajna and a means to achieving it. The order in which the Buddha states the six paramitas—generosity, restraint, patience, diligence, concentration, and wisdom—accurately reveals the stages of growth that one goes through as one moves from initial intuition toward full realization of the truth. The Buddha often describes this path as a one of purification.

The *Sutra of Perfect Enlightenment* says, "When the deluded mind has ceased to be, the dust of delusion will also cease to be." Master Hui Neng said, "Prajna paramita arises out of perfect purity." Nagarjuna said, "When no dharmas arise, prajna arises."

A pure heart is a compassionate heart. A pure mind is concerned about others. When compassion and purity are complete, the mind naturally becomes disentangled from all lakshana. The *Heart Sutra* speaks from this level of awareness when it says, "Form is emptiness, emptiness is form." This says two things, both of them equally important. Form is emptiness: things are not what they seem. Emptiness is form: and yet what they seem is where we are.

The *Treatise on the Perfection of Great Wisdom* says, "The heart of prajna lies both in going beyond all dharmas and in being within all dharmas." Prajna is not a means of escaping from this world; it is full understanding of what this world really is. Prajna is in this world completely and yet it is not of this world at all. The *Vimalakirtinirdesha Sutra* alludes to this when it says, "Life and death are one with nirvana."

Master Ching K'ung said, "Prajna means having wisdom about the essential nature of all things. It is what a buddha sees and knows.... [The] teachings of the Buddha, which are meant to lead all sentient beings to enlightenment, are known as prajna writings." He also says, "Sentient beings know that all dharmas arise from conditions, but they do not see the deep nature of these conditions; thus they chase after lakshana and become confused. All buddhas know that the deep nature of all conditions is emptiness. They know that conditions exist, and yet at the same time, they know that they do not have any absolute existence; and thus they are enlightened."

Chiang Wei-nung said, "Concerning all dharmas, there are four basic things that can be said about them—they have being, they do not have being, they both have and do not have being, they both do not have and do not not have being. Deep prajna is beyond these four statements; it is that which is left after all refutations have been made."

Sun Chien-feng said, "Prajna is entirely different and distinct from ordinary intelligence. Prajna is purity without defilement."

The *Sutra of Complete Enlightenment* says, "As long as there is introspection and enlightenment, there are still obstructions."

The *Treatise on the Perfection of Great Wisdom* says, "Prajna gives birth to all buddhas and it empowers all bodhisattvas. The Buddha-dharma is prajna."

The *Mahaprajnaparamita Sutra* says that there are ten benefits to be gained from studying and practicing the Buddha's prajna teachings. These are:

1. The ability to be generous without being attached to the form or the act of giving.
2. The ability to be moral without clinging to moral rules.
3. The ability to be patient without having the thought that one is being patient.
4. The ability to be diligent without giving thought to one's "self."
5. The ability to attain deep samadhi states without becoming overly entranced by them.
6. The ability to be untouched by demonic forces.
7. The ability to hear wrong teachings without becoming agitated.
8. The ability to cross the river of life and death and reach nirvana.
9. The ability to continually increase one's feelings of compassion for other sentient beings.
10. The ability to dedicate one's life to the Mahayana way.

Prajna is perfect awareness of the unity of the self with all things. It is the source of all goodness and the substance of all enlightenment. Prajna is difficult to explain because it is a self-awareness that dissolves the self; it is a wisdom that is so deep it no longer has a one-pointed frame of reference. Even the Buddha cannot just hand it to us; he can only show us how to attain it for ourselves. The *Upasakashila Sutra* says that there are three basic ways to make progress toward gaining prajna wisdom: the first is to hear the truth, the second is to contemplate the truth, and the third is to practice the truth.

EMPTINESS

Prajna teaches us that nothing should be clung to because there is nothing that can be clung to. Everything is empty. Nothing is absolute. In this short section I will mention some of the ways that Buddhist thinkers have conceived of emptiness:

1. The two emptinesses. These are the most basic concepts of emptiness in Mahayana Buddhism. The two emptinesses are the emptiness of people and the emptiness of all dharmas. In this view, the idea that there is a self or a soul living somewhere inside of the body is an illusion that arises from the existence of the body and nothing more. Thus, people are empty. At the same time, all dharmas are empty because all dharmas are produced by a convergence of many causes, and thus none of them has an absolute being or nature of its own.
2. The three emptinesses. Sentient beings are empty, the Dharma is empty, all things are empty. This is essentially the view presented in the *Diamond Sutra.*
3. The four emptinesses. The *Mahasamnipata Sutra* describes four kinds of emptiness: the emptiness of all lakshana, the emptiness of all no-lakshana, the emptiness of all self-generated lakshana, and the emptiness of all other-generated lakshana.

4. The six emptinesses. The *Shariputrabhidharma Shastra* says that there are six basic kinds of emptiness: a) inner emptiness, or the emptiness of the six sense organs; b) outer emptiness, or the emptiness of the data that the sense organs receive; c) inner and outer emptiness, or the consequent emptiness of the body; d) empty emptiness, or the emptiness of all concepts of emptiness; e) great emptiness, or the emptiness of the entire universe; and f) supreme emptiness, or the emptiness of anything beyond the universe.

5. The *Abhidharmamahavibhasa Shastra* says that there are ten basic kinds of emptiness: a) inner emptiness; b) outer emptiness; c) inner and outer emptiness; d) the emptiness of conditioned dharmas; e) the emptiness of unconditioned dharmas; f) the emptiness of dispersal and disintegration; g) the emptiness of self-nature; h) the emptiness of limits or borders; i) supreme emptiness; and j) the emptiness of emptiness.

There are many other analyses of emptiness in Buddhist literature. The ones mentioned here should suffice to give the reader an idea of how this word is used by Buddhists. The most important things to understand about emptiness are: (1) it is not a negative or discouraging term, but a conceptual means to understanding the truth; (2) it should not lead one toward a life of inactivity or isolation; and (3) it must be integrated with compassion. Emptiness without compassion can be a terrible trap; rather than lead one toward prajna, it may actually lead one away from it.

9 The Four Fruits Are Empty

"Subhuti, what do you say? Would it be right for[50] *a shrotapana*[51] *to think like this: 'I have attained the fruit of*[52] *a shrotapana'?"*

Subhuti said, "No, World-honored One. And why is this? Shrotapana means 'stream-enterer,' and yet there is nothing to be entered. Indeed, to not enter into form, sound, smell, taste, touch, or thought is what is called shrotapana."

"Subhuti, what do you say? Would it be right for a sakradagami[53] *to think like this: 'I have attained the fruit of a sakradagami'?"*

Subhuti said, "No, World-honored One. And why is this? Sakradagami means 'once-returner,' and yet in truth there is no such thing as returning.[54] *This is what is called sakradagami."*

"Subhuti, what do you say? Would it be right for an anagami[55] *to think like this: 'I have attained the fruit of an anagami'?"*

Subhuti said, "No, World-honored One. And why is this? Anagami means 'never-returner,' and yet in truth there is no such thing as never returning. This is the reason it is called anagami."

"Subhuti, what do you say? Would it be right for an arahant [56]
to think like this: 'I have attained the path of an arahant'?"

Subhuti said, "No, World-honored One. And why is this? There
is no dharma called 'arahant.' World-honored One, if an arahant
were to think 'I have attained the path of an arahant,' then he would
be clinging to self, human being, sentient being, and soul. [57]

"World-honored One, the Buddha has said that I have attained [58]
nondisputational samadhi, [59] *and that among all people, I am the*
best in this; and that among all arahants, I am also the best at going
beyond desire. And yet, I do not have the thought that I am an
arahant that has gone beyond desire. World-honored One, if I were to
have the thought that I had attained the path of an arahant, then the
World-honored One would not have said that Subhuti takes delight in
the practice of aranya. Since Subhuti is wholly without any practice,
Subhuti has been said to take delight in the practice of aranya." [60]

In section seven, the Buddha led Subhuti to say, "The Dharma of which
the Tathagata speaks cannot be held onto, it cannot be spoken, it is not
a law, and it is not a non-law." This statement teaches us not to cling to
any concept or formula concerning the Dharma; the Dharma is a way
to do something, it is not itself the thing that is done. People sometimes
say that the *Diamond Sutra* is an "abstract" teaching. Nothing could be
further from the truth; in this sutra, the Buddha is specifically teaching
us how to find a way past abstractions. In section eight, the Buddha
emphasizes the importance of these teachings by saying that all buddhas are "born of this sutra." He also reiterates one of his main themes

by saying, "the Buddhadharma is not the Buddhadharma." If we were to reword this phrase by using earlier statements, we might say, "All lakshana, including all lakshana of the Buddhadharma, are delusive." Throughout this sutra, the Buddha is very clear about telling us that nothing can be clung to.

In section nine, the Buddha observes the four basic stages of the Buddhist path from the point of view of someone who has achieved all of the fruits of that path. From this vantage, he leads Subhuti to say that there is no path, there is no fruit of the path, and there is no one who actually traverses the path. In the *Diamond Sutra*, the Buddha is principally speaking to bodhisattvas, people or beings who have dedicated their lives to the service of others. While all bodhisattvas are dedicated to the well-being of others, it is important to remember that they must also take care of themselves, for if one is unable to swim, one will find it difficult to save those who are drowning. The path of "four fruits" mentioned in this section is the path of self-saving. In later sections the bodhisattva path will be taken up again; in those sections, the Buddha will again say that there is no one to be saved, no such thing as saving, and no one who actually does the saving. In this section, the Buddha mentions the path of self-saving for two basic reasons: (1) to be complete and unequivocal in his teaching, and (2) to remove any possibility that his discussion of the bodhisattva path might be misinterpreted to mean that it is the wrong path.

Another interpretation of this passage is that the Buddha is directing his comments at those who have dedicated themselves to achieving liberation for themselves alone. People like this sometimes fall into the mistaken belief that their practice is actually going to lead them out of this world. They misunderstand the metaphor of "crossing the ocean of life and death" to mean that one actually goes to some other place when one becomes enlightened. All of the Buddha's prajna teachings, including the *Diamond Sutra*, state emphatically that this is a false belief. Prajna wisdom is based on understanding that this world and nirvana are conjoined; nirvana is another way of seeing this world. Enlightenment occurs here, not somewhere else.

The *Mahaparinirvana Sutra* makes this point by saying that true wisdom lies in an enlightened synthesis of all dualistic pairs. The sutra says: "The wise understand that clarity and darkness do not have separate natures; their true natures are nondualistic. Deluded people make absolute distinctions between good and evil, between the doable and the undoable, between a good path and a bad path, between black dharmas and white dharmas, while those who are wise clearly understand that these pairs do not have separate natures. The true nature of all things is nondualistic."

In the *Pravaradevaraja Paripriccha Sutra,* King Pravaradeva asks the Buddha how to overcome hindrances to achieving perfect purity of mind. The Buddha answers him as follows: "Great king, this is something that can be known but not described in words. And why is this? This truth is beyond words, beyond language, beyond all speech. It is not a mere discussion, it is not this, it is not that, it is devoid of lakshana, it has no lakshana. It is beyond thought, beyond sensation, beyond contemplation, beyond mental activity, and without lakshana. It is beyond all duality, beyond all delusion, beyond all demonic activity, beyond hindrance and danger. It is not something that can be merely known about. It has no location. It is perfectly tranquil. It is realized by sages. It is found by entering the wisdom realm that transcends all distinctions. It has no self, and no attributes of a self. If you seek it, you cannot find it. It is not something to be grasped, and it is not something to be let go of. It is without stain, without defilement. It is pure and beyond all corruption. It is supreme, the highest. Its nature is eternal and never changes. Whether a buddha appears in the world or not, its nature abides forever."

NONDISPUTATIONAL SAMADHI

The phenomenal world is composed of paired opposites; hot and cold, left and right, male and female, good and evil, and so on. When we cling to one side of a dualistic pair, we often become argumentative. Nondisputational samadhi arises when we no longer cling to any of the attributes of duality. Master P'u Wan makes this comment about disputes and nondisputes: "The ancients always said that disputes arise from a mind that wants to be victorious, thus turning its back on the true path. The word *nondisputational* means no self, no person, no this, no that, no high, no low, no saintliness, and no ordinariness. When people grasp at anything, they cause a dualistic relationship to come into being and give themselves reasons to have disputes, and thus they become overwhelmingly attached to life and death." He continues with this advice: "And what is the way to free oneself from this? Do not allow the things of this world to defile your mind, and do not trouble other sentient beings. In this way, you will achieve the nondisputational state."

10 Making the Buddha Realm Magnificent

The Buddha said to Subhuti, "What do you say? When the Tathagata
was in the realm of Dipankara Buddha,[61] *did he gain anything by his*
practice of the Dharma?"

"No, World-honored One, when the Tathagata was in the realm of
Dipankara Buddha, he did not gain anything from his practice of the
Dharma."

"Subhuti, what do you say? Does a bodhisattva make a buddha
realm magnificent?"[62]

"No, World-honored One. And why is this? That which makes a
buddha realm magnificent is not magnificent,[63] *and this is what is*
called magnificence."[64]

"For this reason, Subhuti, all great bodhisattvas should give rise
to purity of mind[65] *in this way: they should give rise to a mind that*
is not based on form, and they should give rise to a mind that is not
based on sound, smell, taste, touch, or thought. They should give rise
to a mind that is not based on anything.

"Subhuti, what do you say? If a man's body were as large as Mount Sumeru,[66] would that body be large?"[67]

Subhuti said, "Very large, World-honored One. And why is this? The Buddha has said that no body is what is called the large body."[68]

This section contains one of the most famous lines in the *Diamond Sutra:* "A bodhisattva should give rise to a mind that is not based on anything." This sentence can be understood in many ways. It can mean: "The consciousness of a bodhisattva should not cling to anything"; or "The awareness of a bodhisattva should not arise from any base"; or "The mind of a bodhisattva should arise from nothing"; or "A bodhisattva should discover that true consciousness has no foundation outside itself"; or "The true consciousness of a bodhisattva arises only within consciousness itself and should not be based upon anything else"; or "The awareness of a bodhisattva should not abide in anything." Some of these renderings drift from the literal meaning of this line, but all of them cluster around the same basic idea. Readers of the *Diamond Sutra* must decide for themselves what this line really means. At its simplest level, it counsels us not to become attached to anything. At a deeper level, it tells us that there is nothing to become attached to anyway. At a level deeper still it says that the foundation of consciousness cannot be found outside itself, that it is not based on anything else. At the deepest level of all, it says that the foundation of consciousness is the level of the Tathagata, and that the Tathagata cannot be found in its fullness at any other level. Enlightenment is full realization of the truth contained in this line, while delusion is nothing more than an endless misunderstanding of it.

In section nine, the Buddha explained the emptiness of the path that one walks for oneself, leading Subhuti to say, "If an arahant were to think 'I have attained the path of an arahant,' then he would be clinging to self, human being, sentient being, and soul." In this section, the

Buddha directs his words at bodhisattvas. He makes it very clear that not even a buddha should believe that there is any perceptual reward of any kind to be gained from the practices taught by the Buddha. Enlightenment does not mean going to some other place, nor does it mean gaining anything in this place.

Though the line, "a bodhisattva should give rise to a mind that is not based on anything," contains a core teaching of the *Diamond Sutra*, it would be a mistake to assume that it is the only teaching in the sutra. In subsequent sections, the Buddha will show that groundlessness is only one aspect of the enlightened mind. There is no Buddhist teaching that does not touch every part of our beings. Philosophically understanding that the mind has no absolute foundation can never be a substitute for actually awakening within the fullness of that mind. The *Diamond Sutra* says nothing if it does not say that.

Incidentally, the great Ch'an master, Hui Neng, is reported to have become enlightened when he heard a man on a street corner recite the line, "give rise to a mind that is not based on anything." In the Chinese tradition, this account has contributed to the line's fame.

NON-ATTACHMENT

The Buddha begins this section by asking Subhuti, "When the Tathagata was in the realm of Dipankara Buddha, did he gain anything by his practice of the Dharma?" Subhuti answers that he did not. One of the Buddha's reasons for repeating this point is to emphasize the importance of non-attachment. All lakshana, both mental and physical, are delusive; to cling to any of them through a false belief that there is something to be gained anywhere is only to perpetuate a state of delusion. One cannot become liberated from delusion by clinging to anything. The *Mahaprajnaparamita Sutra* says, "Great bodhisattvas are able to cross from this shore to the other shore by virtue of their ability not to cling to any dharma whatsoever. If there is the slightest clinging to any dharma, it is not possible to cross to the other shore."

The "other shore" is a metaphor for liberation; it does not mean that one leaves this world or goes somewhere when one is liberated. The key to understanding this aspect of prajna wisdom is to understand that non-attachment creates a huge *gestalt* shift; if one can be perfectly non-attached for just a moment, the whole world will suddenly look different. This change is both the source and the beginning of the enlightened consciousness of an awakened being.

The Buddha taught non-attachment not as a means of escaping reality, but as a means of dealing with the fundamental nature of reality. There simply is nothing to which we can attach ourselves, no matter how hard we try. The idea of behaving without attachment springs from understanding that everything is empty. The self is empty, the desires of the self are empty, and the objects of those desires also are empty. In time, things will change and the conditions that produced our current desires will be gone. Why then, cling to them now? The Buddha taught that our tendency to cling to the illusion of permanence is a fundamental cause of suffering. In the *Diamond Sutra*, he raises this basic argument to its highest form.

In the *Sutra of the Secret Treasures of the Tathagata* the Buddha addresses Mahakashyapa, one of his principal disciples, saying, "Mahakashyapa, how is one to realize that defilement arises from causes and conditions? Realize that all conditioned dharmas are without a self-nature, and that, indeed, nothing has truly arisen [when they arise]." Conditioned dharmas are all of the things that we normally think of as being real, or as having some sort of self-nature of their own. All phenomena perceived by our six senses are conditioned dharmas. With such statements, the Buddha strikes at the heart of human psychology, for almost all people think and act as if their worlds were composed of absolute entities. One of the principal goals of the Buddha's prajna teachings is to undo our almost instinctive tendency to perceive ourselves as having some absolute essence that must have this or that right now. These teachings are both philosophical and fundamentally practical. The Buddha is trying to help us change, so that our suffering can end. Nothing is to be "gained" by understanding what he is saying, but we will change completely and be free from the cycles of delusion that determine the lives of all unenlightened sentient beings.

The *Shurangama Sutra* says, "It is hard for sentient beings to follow the right path because they are both argumentative and stubborn. Argumentation arises from attachment, attachment arises from the tendency to make distinctions among things, and the tendency to make distinctions among things arises from having a strong ego. The Buddhadharma was designed to correct these problems."

MAGNIFICENCE

Following Subhuti's answer that the Tathagata did not gain anything by his practice of the Dharma, the Buddha asks him, "Subhuti, what do you say? Does a bodhisattva make a buddha realm magnificent?" He might also have asked, does a bodhisattva really do anything that improves the buddha realm he lives in? Is there any perceptible value at all to a bodhisattva? Not surprisingly, Subhuti answers that there is not. He says that a bodhisattva cannot make a buddha realm magnificent because it is "the absence of magnificence that is truly magnificent." This point squares the circle; no one anywhere can claim anything or cling to anything. The Buddha himself gained nothing by his practice of the Dharma. Bodhisattvas not only gain nothing for themselves, they do nothing to improve the realms in which they reside. This point recalls the third section when the Buddha says that a bodhisattva "should realize as [he vows] to save all sentient beings that in truth there are no sentient beings to be saved." There can be no mistaking this line now; not only are there no sentient beings to be saved, but there is nothing to be gained for oneself, and there is nothing that can be construed as a contribution to the buddha realm in which one lives.

A *buddha realm* is a world system that is conditioned and informed by the buddha who presides over it. Our world system is the buddha realm of Shakyamuni Buddha. In some Buddhist sutras, bodhisattvas are said to make buddha realms "magnificent" by their practice of the six paramitas. In the *Diamond Sutra*, the Buddha denies the possibility of any such magnificence. The Buddha taught on many different levels. If in one sutra he says that the six paramitas are "magnificent" while in another he says that they are not, he is not contradicting himself. He is simply rising to a higher level of truth to suit his audience. We can be certain that the *Diamond Sutra* teaches a very high level of truth because this discourse is directed at Subhuti, the Buddha's foremost disciple in wisdom.

Master P'u Wan says of these lines, "A buddha realm is nothing more than a realm of pure mind; it is born of emptiness and resolved in purity. If we can make our minds pure, then [our] buddha realm will be pure. And thus [Subhuti says that a bodhisattva] does not [make a buddha realm magnificent]."

He also says, "That which is called magnificence is a synthesis of two truths—true emptiness does not obstruct anything within the phenomenal universe, and nothing within the phenomenal universe obstructs true emptiness. Though this magnificence is based on real principles, it is not something that can ever be gotten hold of or attained." Master P'u Wan adds that the Buddha discusses magnificence just before his statement that "a bodhisattva should give rise to a mind that is not based on anything" because this emphasizes the truth that there is nothing more magnificent or better than giving rise to a mind that is not based on anything.

NOT BASED ON ANYTHING

Master P'u Wan says that "not based on anything" refers to true emptiness, while "give rise to a mind" refers to the wondrous variety of being. He continues, "The combination of 'not being based on anything' and 'giving rise to a mind' means that ultimate truth and conventional reality are brought together and synthesized, thus becoming the supreme truth of the middle path."

He also says, "The pure, true mind that is not based on anything is used everyday by everyone, and yet, due to their confusions, almost no one knows this mind. The World-honored One uses metaphors and words to help sentient beings understand and know this mind."

THREE TRUTHS

Buddhism is sometimes called the "middle way" or the "middle path." It is called this for several reasons: (1) because the Buddha taught that one should be neither too strict nor too lax in one's spiritual practice; (2) because the Dharma teaches a truth that lies between eternalism and nihilism; and (3) because it teaches a synthesis between the emptiness of phenomenal reality and the validity of that reality. Here we shall briefly discuss the third reason.

The synthesis of emptiness and phenomenal reality is often called the "three truths" because it is composed of three basic terms: (1) phenomenal reality, (2) the emptiness of phenomenal reality, and (3) the union of these two.

Phenomenal reality means everything that we perceive with our six senses—everything that we see, feel, hear, taste, touch, think, dream, imagine, analyze, or cognize in any way. The first truth is sometimes also called "relative truth" because it describes the realm of duality, wherein all things are interconnected, and wherein each of them exists only in relation to other things.

The second of the three truths, the emptiness of phenomenal reality, has been discussed in other sections. Remember, when we say that phenomenal reality is empty, we are not saying that it does not exist. We are simply saying that it is always changing. Nothing within it has a permanent self-nature. Nothing within it is ultimately or permanently real. The third truth is the union or synthesis of the first two.

Throughout the long history of Chinese Buddhism, Chinese masters have repeatedly emphasized that ultimate truth can only be understood in terms of the three truths and that the three truths must be taken together. Taken together, the three truths describe a whole that is greater than the sum of its parts. They reveal the middle way, the perfect balance between practice and understanding, intellect and emotion, wisdom and activity. The three truths readily lend themselves to misunderstanding when viewed from only one side at a time. When we place too much emphasis on the truth of phenomenal reality, we tend to cling to that reality and cause ourselves suffering. When we place too much emphasis on the emptiness of phenomenal reality, we tend to become cold or indecisive. When we place too much emphasis on the synthesis of these two truths, we may miss the immediacy and importance of both of them.

All of the Buddha's teachings are fundamentally practical. The three truths are at once levels of practical understanding and levels of philosophical verity. In the *Diamond Sutra* the Buddha is presenting precise instructions to Subhuti about how a bodhisattva should behave and how he should understand his own mind. This union of behavior and understanding is the core of the Buddha's prajna teachings.

There are many statements in the *Diamond Sutra* that can be interpreted as three-truths statements. These statements have the basic form: "x is not x and so it is called x." In these kinds of statements, the first term—"x"—stands for the first of the three truths, phenomenal reality. The second term—"not x"—stands for the second of the three truths, the emptiness of phenomenal reality. And the third term—"and so it is called x"—stands for the last of the three truths, the synthesis of the first two.

The first instance of a three-truths statement in the *Diamond Sutra* occurs in section three, when the Buddha says, "All great bodhisattvas…should realize as they vow to save all sentient beings that in truth there are no sentient beings to be saved." The first truth is "sentient beings," the second truth is "no sentient beings," and the third truth is the union of these two, for great bodhisattvas "vow to save" them anyway.

The second clear example of a statement of the three truths occurs in section five, when the Buddha says, "All lakshana are delusive. If you can see that all lakshana are not lakshana, then you will see the Tathagata." The first term of this statement—"all lakshana"—stands for phenomenal reality, while the second term—"are not lakshana"—stands for the ultimate emptiness of that reality. The third term in this sequence—"then you will see the Tathagata"—is the enlightened synthesis of the first two terms. The Tathagata, the enlightened buddha mind, can be found when the perfect synthesis of phenomenal reality and its emptiness is attained.

The third clear example of a three-truths statement in the *Diamond Sutra* occurs in section eight, when Subhuti says, "This goodness is devoid of a 'goodness nature,' and therefore the Tathagata would say that it is great." The first term—"this goodness"—is the first truth; the second term—"devoid of a 'goodness nature'"—is the second truth; while the last term—"it is great"—is the synthesis, the third truth.

In this section, Subhuti's statement—"That which makes a buddha realm magnificent is not magnificent, and this is what is called magnificence."—can also be interpreted as a three-truths statement. The first term—"magnificent"—is what we normally think of as virtuous behavior, the second term—"not magnificent"—is the emptiness of that behavior, and the third term—"and that is what is called magnificence"—is the synthesis of the first two. Each level is true in its own way. Ultimate reality can only be apprehended, however, when all three levels are taken at once.

The first two elements of the three truths—phenomenal reality and the emptiness of that reality—can also be understood as dualistic opposites, possessing a similar, though grander, nature than the paired opposites of hot and cold, male and female, good and bad, or up and down. Highest complete enlightenment is often described as being a state that is beyond all duality, including the duality of phenomenon and the emptiness of phenomenon. When the Buddha says in section twenty-three that highest complete enlightenment is "equal and without high or low," he is saying, in part, that it is beyond all duality and all distinctions that can be formed by the phenomenal mind.

While the three truths can be a powerful tool to help us understand the *Diamond Sutra*, we should not allow this method of interpretation to become our only way of understanding this teaching. As the sutra says, "all lakshana are delusive." If the three truths become a lakshana that filters our comprehension of the sutra, they may actually cause us to miss the very deepest levels of its meaning. The three truths should be used, but they should not be overused. They are a comparatively easy way to remind us of where the keys to ultimate reality are. It would be an extreme oversimplification, however, to believe that they are themselves the keys, much less ultimate reality itself.

In the *Vimalakirtinirdesha Sutra*, there is a famous exchange between Shakyamuni Buddha and Shariputra. Shariputra asks the Buddha why other buddha realms are so much more beautiful than his. The Buddha replies by tapping his foot on the ground. In an instant the world around them becomes as beautiful and magnificent as anything that Shariputra can imagine. The Buddha then says, "Shariputra, my buddha realm is fundamentally pure and magnificent. In order to educate lower beings, however, it appears to be filled with impurities...Shariputra, if your mind is pure, you will see that this world is perfectly magnificent and that it contains no defilements at all." The world—phenomenal reality, the first truth—looks bad to Shariputra because he cannot see its fundamental emptiness, the second truth. With the Buddha's help, he gains a brief vision of the third truth, ultimate reality.

The magnificence of this world is revealed whenever we participate in it positively. At an ordinary level, we can contribute to its magnificence by building temples and helping others meet their material needs. At a higher level, we can contribute by exhibiting compassion in everything we do. At a level higher still, we can contribute to the magnificence of this world by remaining secure in our knowledge that this world is nothing more than a reflection of our own minds; in truth, it is already magnificent and does not require us to seek anything beyond it.

THE DEEPEST VOW

The Buddha directs his famous line—"a bodhisattva should give rise to a mind that is not based on anything"—at bodhisattvas, beings who have vowed to dedicate their lives to the service of others. In this context, his words can be understood both philosophically and practically. The full line says, "All great bodhisattvas should give rise to purity of mind in this way: they should give rise to a mind that is not based on form, and they should give rise to a mind that is not based on sound, smell, taste, touch, or thought. They should give rise to a mind that is not based on anything." Pure consciousness has no foundation. The enlightenment of a Buddha contains everything and thus it has no base.

Master P'u Wan says, "If the mind of a bodhisattva has even the slightest thought of attaching itself to some base, then it contains a defilement and cannot be called pure."

The *Visheshachintabrahma Paripriccha Sutra* describes a vision of a mind that does not base itself on anything when it says, "All dharmas are equal, nothing interacts with anything, there is no going beyond birth and death, there is no nirvana."

In the *Mahaparinirvana Sutra* the Buddha describes the elusive nature of awakened consciousness with a beautiful series of metaphors. He says, "Good people, it is like looking into the distant sky at a bird flying; at one moment it seems that nothing is there, at another moment it seems that there is a bird flying. One is not sure, but it seems as if one has seen something. Bodhisattvas perceive their buddha nature in much this same way; they only see a small part of it. Others do not see it at all. Good people, it is like a drunk walking; he sees the path only through a haze of confusion. Bodhisattvas perceive their buddha nature in much this same way; they only see a small part of it. Others do not see it at all. Good people, it is like a person far away at sea. Far in the distance he thinks he can see the shape of a large ship, but he is not sure if it is a ship or if it is just nothing at all. After a while, he becomes certain that it is indeed a ship. Bodhisattvas perceive their buddha nature in much this same way. Good people, it is like a man walking home at night. Suddenly there is a flash of lightning that causes him to think that he has seen a group of cows, but he is not sure if they were really cows or if they were just shadows in the mist. After peering into the dark for a long time, he determines that it must be a group of cows that he has seen, and yet he is not completely sure. Bodhisattvas perceive the buddha nature that lies within them in much this same way; they are not completely sure about what they are seeing. Good people, it is like a person on a dark night looking at a painting of a bodhisattva. At first he thinks that he might be seeing a real bodhisattva, but after a while he realizes that he is probably only looking at a painting of a bodhisattva, and yet he is not completely sure of that either. Bodhisattvas perceive the buddha nature that lies within them in much this same way; they are not completely sure about what they are seeing."

The full Sanskrit title of the *Diamond Sutra* is the *Vajracchedika Prajnaparamita Sutra,* or the "Diamond that Cuts Through Illusion to the Perfection of Wisdom Sutra." These teachings are meant to cut through ignorance. As we follow the Buddha's argument, we realize that he is cutting through everything we have ever believed in. As his diamond cuts deeper, we realize that we are losing yet another part of our false selves. The Buddha is like a doctor who cuts away the bandages of ignorance once our wound is healed; he is like a friend who cuts the fetters of delusion from our feet and lets us walk again. What is true freedom? Can it be found in greed, anger, or ignorance? Is not true freedom, the freedom of pure awareness unobstructed by delusion? The *Diamond Sutra* shows the way to perfect liberation. At first we are like drunks stumbling in the night as we try to understand it, but in time the wisdom sun rises and the path stretches before us with stunning clarity.

Buddhism is based on the intelligent unity of compassion and wisdom. The Buddha said that compassion without wisdom is as dangerous as wisdom without compassion. Compassion without wisdom may cause more harm than good, while wisdom without compassion can quickly lead to arrogance and selfish isolation from the needs of others. The teachings in the *Diamond Sutra* are directed at bodhisattvas who have vowed to dedicate their lives to others. We must never make the mistake of thinking that when the diamond of prajna has cut away the last strand of delusion, nothing is left, for the world will still be here. There will still be the need to live and to behave. There will always be the need for compassion. Consider this Ch'an poem:

> *Before samadhi, the mountains were mountains*
> *and the streams were streams.*
> *In samadhi, the mountains were not mountains*
> *and the streams were not streams.*
> *After samadhi, the mountains were mountains*
> *and the streams were streams again.*

11 The Unconditioned Is Supreme

"Subhuti, if each grain of sand in the Ganges River were to become

a Ganges River, and if the sand in all of those rivers were added up,

what do you say? Would that be a lot of sand?"

Subhuti said, "It would be very much, World-honored One.

The number of Ganges Rivers alone would be enormous; the amount

of sand would be even greater than that."

"Subhuti, I am going to speak the truth to you now: if a good man

or a good woman were to give away as many great chiliocosms of precious

jewels⁶⁹ as all of those grains of sand, would his goodness be great?"

Subhuti said, "It would be very great, World-honored One."

The Buddha said to Subhuti, "If a good man or a good woman

receives and upholds as few as four verses of this sutra, and if he teaches it

to others, then his goodness will be greater than that."

Prince Chao Ming's title for this section uses the term *wu wei*. In Taoism, *wu wei* means "non-action." Taoist non-action connotes the "wisdom" of water, the wisdom to flow and not resist what is happening. Early Buddhist translators in China used this term to translate the Sanskrit word *asamskrta*. *Asamskrta* is usually rendered in English as the "unconditioned" or "uncreated." It means that which is not affected by causes or conditions. All phenomena and all dharmas in the universe are affected by causes and conditions. Only enlightenment is unconditioned. In the *Mahaparinirvana Sutra*, the Buddha says that nirvana is immortal: "It is a good light, like the summer sun, a body without borders." The Tathagata, the original buddha mind, buddha nature, enlightenment, original mind, original purity, purity of mind, a mind that arises from no base—all of these refer to the same thing. All of these words refer to the unconditioned state of the Tathagata. Though the Buddha also advocated a kind of Taoist *wu wei* in many circumstances, it would be a mistake to equate Taoist non-action with the Buddhist "unconditioned."

Just as Chinese translators sometimes used preexisting Chinese terms to express Buddhist ideas in Chinese, so English translators sometimes have used preexisting English words to express Buddhist ideas in English. Most of these borrowings cause little or no confusion; "phenomenon" stands in quite well for "dharma," "enlightenment" works for "bodhi," "meditate" is very close to the word "samadhi." The occasional misconception that arises from the use of such near-equivalents can usually be cleared up with an extra sentence or two. Nevertheless, the choice of a word sometimes causes a lot of confusion. Probably the greatest single misunderstanding of Buddhist ideas in English surrounds the word *nirvana*. Literally, *nirvana* means "extinguished" or "gone out." The Buddha used this term to describe enlightenment because in the enlightened state, there is no suffering, there are no obstacles, there is no fear, and there are no defilements; all of them have been extinguished. Nirvana is changeless, immortal, infinite, unobstructed, endless. Even in English, we use "negative" terms to describe this ultimate state. We say it is not mortal, not finite, not changeable, not obstructed, not defiled. Nirvana is beyond anything that we can think of. It is so vast and so great, we have no words except negative ones to say what it is. Just as we have few terms in English with which to "grasp" a state that is wholly beyond our present state of awareness, so people in ancient India were unable to grasp nirvana with the words available then. Thus, the Buddha frequently used negative terms to evoke some idea of what enlightenment is.

If his use of negative terms like "deathless" or "extinguished" to describe nirvana leads us into believing that *nirvana* means "nothingness," we have made a big mistake. Buddhism is not a nihilistic religion. *Nirvana* does not mean "nothing." The Buddha took great pains to show that nirvana is a state marked by compassion and joy, as well as by the absence of all conditioned phenomena. The Buddha frequently used negative descriptions of nirvana because he did not want his listeners to mistake nirvana for what they already knew. If he said that nirvana is joyful, they might think of an earthly joy. If he said that nirvana was eternal, they might think that it was something that lasted for a very long time, rather than something that was completely beyond time. Most of us only glimpse nirvana. It is a flash of light that is gone as soon as it appears. It is like a bird in the distant sky; we think we see it, and then we are not sure. Since we are like drunks stumbling along a path at night, the Buddha said over and over that nirvana is an end to delusion. It is sobriety, awakening, the sun that rises in the morning. It is not the night, the haze, the confused elements of consciousness that we experience as we stumble along in our usual and present state.

This section reemphasizes the importance of consciousness over any act of material generosity. Prince Chao Ming titled this section "The Unconditioned Is Supreme" to suggest the ultimate state of nirvana that can be found by studying the *Diamond Sutra*. The unconditioned state, true to its name, is not conditioned by anything; it is beyond all dualities of hot and cold, male and female, good and bad, joy and sorrow, and so on. It is beyond duality itself. It is supreme, above all other states. There is nothing better or greater than the enlightened state of the Tathagata. This state cannot be bought; it must be found. It cannot be borrowed; it must be earned. No matter how much good work one does in this world, one cannot expect to receive enlightenment as a reward. The unconditioned state is an ultimate state of awareness, and therefore it must be attained consciously, by study, by meditation, and by introspection. The Buddha said that all dharmas are marked by both change and nirvana. Like change, nirvana is everywhere. Unlike change, it is perfectly stable.

It is important to remember as we continue reading the *Diamond Sutra* that this world is permeated and subsumed by the unconditioned state. The Buddha did not go anywhere when he entered nirvana; he simply became fully aware of where he was. Nirvana is in this world, but it is not conditioned by this world. It is a different order of awareness.

The *Sadharmasmritiupastana Sutra* says, "All phenomenal things are impermanent. The good Dharma increases wisdom. The things of this world all degenerate. Only the Dharma is solid and lasts." It also says, "Material wealth can always be stolen or destroyed, but Dharma treasures can be stolen neither by kings, nor thieves, nor floods, nor fires."

Wisdom cannot be taken from us. When we increase our wisdom, we alter both our karma and the imperatives of our karma. Wisdom shows us how to react to conditions that we ourselves have caused. Once we understand the fundamental emptiness of all phenomena, we are less likely to become angry or to act in a way that creates bad karma. All bad karma arises from bad intentions. The heart of the universe is intention. When our wisdom leads us to understand this point, we begin to understand that the Buddha became a powerful magnet of consciousness because his intentions were so pure and compassionate. The world around us changes the moment we understand the primacy of our intentions. Good intentions bring good results. Bad intentions bring bad results. The energy of intention is the primary energy in the universe. All other energies are derived from it.

In the *Diamond Sutra*, the Buddha teaches us how to understand the merging of unconditioned awareness with unconditionally compassionate intention. This is not a simple idea. This is the enlightened state. Perfected, this state is the Buddha. At first, we only glimpse this truth as if in a flash of lightning. In time, however, we begin to understand that this flash reveals a mind that is deeper than any phenomenal desire or any conception of mind that we have ever had. In the *Diamond Sutra,* the Buddha leads us toward actually experiencing that revelation. The exquisite skill he exhibits in this sutra is one of the greatest weddings of art, philosophy, and religion in all of world literature. The Buddha leads us through a flash of understanding to an entirely different way of seeing everything.

The *Mahaprajnaparamita Sutra* contains a record of the following exchange between the Buddha and Subhuti: "Subhuti asked the Buddha, 'World-honored One, if a great bodhisattva wants to achieve highest complete enlightenment, how should he behave?'

"The Buddha replied, 'He should learn equanimity and he should practice equanimity of language with all sentient beings; he should not be partial to any one or another of them. And he should be compassionate with all sentient beings, and he should always be compassionate in his use of language. He should form good intentions toward all sentient beings, and he should evince good intentions in his use of language. He should be peaceful and calm with all sentient beings, and he should always be peaceful in his use of language. In his relations with all other sentient beings, he should give rise to a mind that is free of blockage and repression, and the language he uses should be free of blockage and repression. He should not be troublesome in his relations with other sentient beings, and his use of language should not be troublesome. He should be loving and respectful in his relations with other sentient beings, and he should treat them as he would his own family and friends.'"

12 Honoring the True Teaching

"Furthermore, Subhuti, anyone who speaks about this sutra, even as little as only four verses of it, should be honored[70] by people in this world, by those in heaven,[71] and by ashuras[72] as if he were a Buddhist shrine. And anyone who practices the teachings of this sutra with all of his strength, or who reads it, or chants it, should be honored that much more. Subhuti, you should know that such a person already has become accomplished in the highest and rarest of dharmas. Wherever this sutra can be found, there also is the Buddha; and it should be honored as if it were one of his disciples."[73]

In the *Mahaparinirvana Sutra*, the Buddha says that a bodhisattva must base his practice on the three concentrations of "emptiness, absence of lakshana, and intention." In this same sutra, the Buddha also says, "If you can practice compassion with all sentient beings morning and night, you will attain eternal joy." Intention is the core of all conscious life. The Buddha placed great emphasis on this point because it is our intentions that create karma, our intentions that help others, our intentions that lead us away from the delusions of individuality toward the immutable verities of enlightened awareness. The importance of intention can be seen in the Buddha's frequent admonitions to behave "compassionately," or to "act for the benefit of all sentient beings." Ultimately, he called on all of us to *vow* to be compassionate, and to always keep the well-being of others uppermost in our minds. The bodhisattva vow is not based on mere allegiance to a person, a group, or an idea. It is based on purification of intention, for whenever our intentions transcend selfish desires, they begin to partake of the universal compassion of the enlightened mind.

In sum, the *Diamond Sutra* teaches that the mind has no absolute base, but that the intentions of the mind are of paramount importance. These two truths must go hand in hand; they cannot properly be separated from each other without creating immense distortions. Consciousness has no base, but there is such a thing as consciousness. Conscious intention colors and moves everything.

The "Verse of the Seven Buddhas" says:

> *Do no evil ever.*
> *Do good always.*
> *Purify your intentions.*
> *These are the teachings of all buddhas.*

There is no better way to purify your intentions than to share the Dharma with others. Sharing the Dharma with others is the highest form of generosity. In this section of the *Diamond Sutra*, the Buddha praises "anyone who speaks about this sutra." There are several things that should be understood about this statement for it to be fully appreciated. Firstly, this comment is not confined to monks and nuns; the Buddha says specifically, "*Anyone* who speaks about this sutra...should be honored...as if he were a Buddhist shrine." Secondly, the Buddha means that our level of understanding should not stop us from "speaking about this sutra." Though only a buddha can be expected to fully comprehend the teaching of the *Diamond Sutra*, the rest of us should not feel deterred from praising it and encouraging others to study it. Prajna wisdom always has two basic elements: that which reflects on the self, and that which reflects on others. By "speaking about this sutra," we share our wisdom, however limited that may be, with others. Thirdly, our "speaking about this sutra" does not mean that we must explain each and every verse. It only means that we encourage others to read and appreciate the deep meaning of the sutra. Lastly, it does not matter at all where our "speaking about this sutra" takes place. We can do it in a temple, on a street corner, in the mountains, in a coffee shop, in our own homes.

Truth can be transmitted at any time, at any place, by anybody. Whenever we actively and consciously reach out to help others learn the truths of the Dharma, we fulfill one more part of the deep imperative of being. The *Upasakashila Sutra* says that ideally there should be sixteen conditions present for any transmission of the Dharma: (1) There must be enough time to do it. (2) It should be transmitted "mind to mind" or "heart to heart." (3) Truths should be presented in an order that listeners can follow and understand. (4) It should be transmitted cooperatively. (5) Our speech should conform to the deep significance of what we are saying. (6) We should speak with joy. (7) We should follow our intuition. (8) We should not speak lightly of the Dharma. (9) We should not try to scare people with it. (10) To the best of our ability, we should speak in accordance with the true Dharma. (11) Our explanation should benefit both ourselves and others at the same time. (12) Our speech should not be too rambling or disorganized. (13) We should make our points clearly and comprehensively. (14) We should be correct in our bearing and try to speak the truth. (15) We must never allow ourselves to become proud because of what we are saying. (16) We should never expect any reward for our words.

The *Upasakashila Sutra* also mentions sixteen conditions that should be present whenever we listen to a Dharma talk: (1) We should have enough time to listen to the end. (2) We should listen with joy. (3) We should pay close attention to what is being said. (4) We should be respectful. (5) We should not look for faults in the speaker. (6) We should not look for disputes. (7) We should not listen for the purpose of proving ourselves right. (8) We should not look down on the speaker. (9) We should not look down on the Dharma, even if we believe that our understanding is at a "higher" level. (10) We should not look down on ourselves if we think that we do not understand everything that has been said. (11) We should listen with pure minds, and not allow ourselves to be distracted by greed, anger, sleepiness, restlessness, or doubt. (12) We should allow ourselves to be inspired to continue reading on the subject after the talk is finished. (13) We should not allow ourselves to be distracted by form, sound, smell, taste, or touch. (14) We should listen with open minds. (15) We should listen with the idea that our new knowledge will help us help others. (16) We should listen with the idea that ultimately the Dharma will teach us to go beyond all listening.

In the *Mahaprajnaparamita Sutra* the Buddha speaks about the importance of intention. He says that true purity of intention is very rare. He says that many people vow to achieve highest complete enlightenment, but that they are "like the eggs laid by a fish; though there are many of them, few grow to become adults." He also says, "Infinite numbers of sentient beings commit themselves to becoming enlightened, but the ones who follow through are so few it is hardly worth speaking about them." The *Diamond Sutra* teaches that while consciousness has no absolute foundation, it cannot become pure until its intentions are perfectly pure. The clarity of pure consciousness cannot be perceived until all impure intentions have been removed from it. Omniscience cannot be discovered until all remnants of delusive individuality have been eradicated. The "good light" cannot be seen until all shadows of greed, anger, and ignorance have disappeared. "Purify your intentions: these are the teachings of all buddhas."

Ch'an Master Lai Kuo (1881–1953) said, "The mind is the Buddha, and there is no other Buddha. The Buddha is the mind, and there is no other mind."

The ancients used to say, "If you want to end delusion, end it; there is no need to further search for the truth."

13 The Name of This Sutra

At that point, Subhuti asked the Buddha, "World-honored One, what should this sutra be called, and how should we receive it and uphold it?"

The Buddha said to Subhuti, "This sutra is called the Diamond Prajnaparamita, and by this name you should receive it and uphold it. And why is this? Subhuti, the Buddha has said that the perfection of wisdom is not the perfection of wisdom and that that is what is called the perfection of wisdom.[74] Subhuti, what do you say? Does the Tathagata really have some Dharma to speak about?"

Subhuti said to the Buddha, "World-honored One, the Tathagata has nothing to speak about."

"Subhuti, what do you say? Is the fine dust of an entire great chiliocosm a lot of dust or not?"

Subhuti said, "It is a lot, World-honored One."

"Subhuti, the Tathagata says that all of that fine dust is not fine dust, and that that is what is called fine dust. The Tathagata says

that the world is not the world, and that that is what is called the

world. Subhuti, what do you say? Can the Tathagata be seen[75] by

his thirty-two marks?"[76]

"No, World-honored One. And why is this? The Tathagata has

said that the thirty-two marks are not marks, and that that is what

is called thirty-two marks."

"Subhuti, if a good man or a good woman were to practice

generosity[77] with as many lives as there are grains of sand in the

Ganges River, his or her goodness would still not be as great as that

of someone who upheld as few as four verses of this sutra and who

spoke of them to others."

In this section, the Buddha tells Subhuti the name of this sutra, as he continues to emphasize the importance of passing this teaching on to future generations. Those of us who are fortunate enough to be studying the *Diamond Sutra* today should pause for a moment to appreciate the many generations who have come before us, each of them faithfully passing the *Diamond Sutra* on to the next. And, as we recognize our debt to the past, we should also recognize our responsibility to the future. The truth of the Dharma can never be lost, but the literature that teaches people how to find that truth can be lost if each generation does not make an effort to sustain the tradition.

The Sanskrit name for the *Diamond Sutra* is *Vajracchedika Prajnaparamita Sutra*. *Vajracchedika* means "diamond cutting." This sutra is described as "diamond-cutting" because the prajna truths elucidated in it are capable of cutting through all forms of ignorance. In Chinese, the *Diamond Sutra* is called the "Diamond Prajnaparamita Sutra." *Prajnaparamita* means "the perfection of wisdom." The perfection of wisdom is the highest of all of the paramitas because only wisdom can show us how to apply the other five paramitas. In English, this sutra has come to be called simply the *Diamond Sutra*.

Master P'u Wan says that a diamond is used in the title of this sutra because just as a diamond is stronger than other stones, so ultimate wisdom "can overcome all defilements, while there is no defilement that can overcome it." Master Ching K'ung said, "The diamond is used as a metaphor for wisdom because a diamond is the hardest, the sharpest, and the brightest [of all precious stones]."

The work of transforming consciousness into diamond awareness must be done by each and every one of us. No one can do it for us. Subhuti's saying "the Tathagata has nothing to speak about" is another way of saying that ultimate wisdom cannot be contained or conveyed by language. It can only be indicated. Truth must be rediscovered through practice and contemplation. While the Buddha's diamond wisdom cuts through ignorance, we ourselves must make the effort to awaken to the depths of these teachings. In the *Lankavatara Sutra*, the Buddha says, "A great bodhisattva must follow the saintly teachings without picking and choosing what he likes. He must be independent and contemplate his own mind until awakening arrives. He does not become enlightened by the actions of someone else, and thus he must discard conventional analyses and elevate his mind; and so he will enter the realm of the Tathagata. This is the way to practice, and this is the way to achieve saintly wisdom."

THAT IS WHAT IS CALLED
THE PERFECTION OF WISDOM

In the *Mahaparinirvana Sutra*, the Buddha says, "The perfection of wisdom is the great emptiness" and that "great bodhisattvas attain awareness of emptiness and thus live in a vast realm of emptiness." A few lines later the Buddha reiterates that "this vast realm of emptiness" is a state of consciousness. He says that bodhisattvas who dwell in it "do not become greedy or attached to any agreeable form, and they do not become repulsed by any disagreeable form." He continues, "This vast realm of emptiness is so large that it contains no duality. It is able to include all dharmas; for this reason it is also sometimes called the 'vast realm of emptiness and equanimity.' When a bodhisattva dwells in this realm, he is capable of seeing and understanding all dharmas, whether they are actions, or conditions, or the nature of things, or lakshana, or causes, or conditions, or the minds of sentient beings, or roots, or states of samadhi, or kinds of teachings, or enlightened friends, or morality, or acts of generosity; without exception, he knows and sees them all."

Clearly, enlightenment is not death. And clearly it is not life as we usually think of it. The "vast realm of emptiness" is a realm of supreme awareness, a realm that is so large "it includes all dharmas" and "contains no duality." In it, the bodhisattva "is capable of seeing and knowing all dharmas…without exception, he knows and sees them all." Only the six paramitas can lead to this state because only the six paramitas can teach us how to completely purify all of our intentions. Purity of intention coupled with perfect understanding of emptiness equals enlightenment.

The *Diamond Sutra* can be difficult to understand, largely because it is an ultimate teaching. It is a sort of conclusion that can be truly understood only after years of practice and study. It is one thing to speak about perfect equanimity, but it is quite another to actually be in a state of awareness that "includes all dharmas." This is the realm of the Buddha. In the *Diamond Sutra*, the Buddha leads Subhuti toward actually seeing through the eyes of the Tathagata.

Once during the T'ang Dynasty, Prince Liang Wu asked a Ch'an master to explain the *Diamond Sutra* to him. The master came in and sat down, and then he tapped a ruler for silence. Then he got up and left. A monk who was present at the time asked the prince if he had understood the teaching. The prince replied, "I am as mystified by it as if I had fallen five miles into a thick fog." The monk then said, "There is nothing anyone can say about the *Diamond Sutra*. The master revealed the depths of its mysteries by leaving the room altogether."

FINE DUST

Buddhists commonly point to the impermanence and insubstantiality of this world by characterizing it as being composed solely of fine dust. The *Avatamsaka Sutra* says, "All sentient beings are the products of innumerable causes and conditions; could there possibly be another world for any one of them? Enlightened beings reside here, just as deluded beings reside here. Enlightened beings have pure minds and therefore perceive a pure world. Deluded beings have defiled minds and therefore perceive a world made up of fine dust."

"Fine dust" is another way of saying "delusion" because when dust accumulates it obscures the original purity of things. Sometimes Buddhists call this dust "guest dust" because it is not an inherent part of the buddha mind. Just as it takes only a moment to wipe the dust from the surface of a mirror, so it takes only a moment to become enlightened; the moment all defiled intentions are cleared from our consciousness, we will see ourselves in the mirror of perfect truth.

Dust clouds the clarity of the metaphorical pool of enlightened awareness. Just as material things are made of dust, so too are our perceptions and thoughts mere dust. The Buddha explained that lakshana appear in the mind with great rapidity; one lakshana or one thought lasts only one *kshana.* The *Record of Investigations of Mysteries* says, "A kshana is [as long as] one thought. A single snap of the fingers contains sixty kshana." Lakshana rush into the mind and appear before it like clouds of dust; deluded awareness is filled with clouds of dust-like lakshana; impure intentions are based on deluded visions of dust. Dust clouds the mind on all levels; matter is dust, illusion is dust, and thought and perception also are dust. Only the Tathagata sees the "vast realm of emptiness" in which all of this floats in the clarity of perfect awareness.

In this section, the metaphor of fine dust is used to reveal three levels of truth: (1) the false level of ordinary reality that is nothing but dust, (2) the level of emptiness in which that dust has no fundamental reality, and (3) the level of ultimate truth that merges and transcends these two levels. All buddhas dwell at this third level, simultaneously in both ordinary and ultimate awareness. At this level, there is nothing in the ordinary world of dust that they do not understand, and nothing in the realm of emptiness that can disturb their perfected intentions.

IMPERMANENCE

All phenomena are interconnected and dependent on other phenomena. Hence, nothing can remain the same. The Buddha taught that all things within the phenomenal world are constantly changing. Nothing is permanent.

Impermanence is one way to understand emptiness. If all things are impermanent, then none of them can have an unchanging "self-nature," and thus all of them are empty.

The Buddha taught that each and every phenomenon, every dharma, arises, abides, changes, and is extinguished. Nothing stays the same. From moment to moment everything is changing. It is human nature to try to cling to a sense of permanence, but it is futile to do so. The Buddha often spoke about the suffering that arises from this very human tendency. In the *Diamond Sutra* he teaches how to stop clinging to impermanent lakshana without becoming indifferent or careless.

There are many ways of understanding impermanence. Two of the most basic are: (1) momentary impermanence—all phenomena change from moment to moment; and (2) serial impermanence—though some things appear to stay the same over a long period of time, in fact they do not. Human life is an example of serial impermanence. Though we seem to remain the "same person" for our whole lives, in fact we are always changing.

The *Treatise on the Perfection of Great Wisdom* says, "How are we to understand the impermanence of conditioned dharmas?... All conditioned dharmas arise dependent on other dharmas and thus each of them is impermanent. Yesterday it did not exist, but today it does exist. Today it exists, but tomorrow it will not."

GENEROSITY

The first of the six paramitas is generosity. At its most basic level, generosity means doing something that causes other sentient beings to move closer to the truth. In section eleven, the Buddha said that upholding as few as four verses of the *Diamond Sutra* is better than giving away a great chiliocosm full of precious jewels. In this section, he makes the point even more strongly by saying that sacrificing as many lives as there are grains of sand in the Ganges River is not equal to upholding as few as four verses of the *Diamond Sutra*. To uphold the truths in the *Diamond Sutra* is to practice generosity of the highest sort, for the *Diamond Sutra* teaches us how to purify our intentions as we find perfect clarity of consciousness. By upholding as few as four verses of the sutra, we lead others by our example to the heart of the Dharma. The Buddha often said that teaching others the Dharma or leading others to it is the highest form of generosity. As generosity leads us to enlightenment, so one of the deepest truths of this sutra is the sutra itself. To be fully understood, the *Diamond Sutra* must be shared with others.

Generosity is the first of the six paramitas because generosity begins with our recognition of our debt to others. Our lives are wholly dependent on others. Were it not for others, we would not have been born, raised, or educated. Were it not for others, most of us would have no place to live and nothing to eat. The *Diamond Sutra* opens with an image of the Buddha receiving food from others. In the current section he exhorts Subhuti to share the gift of his teaching with others, and by extension, he exhorts all of us to share the wisdom of the Dharma with others. The bodhisattva vow is based on the recognition of our essential unity with all other sentient beings in the universe. This recognition can become a powerful catalyst for change if it inspires in us the companion recognition that our intentions are the deepest and most important level of our interconnectedness to others. When our intentions are pure, we see others as they really are. When our intentions are defiled, we see in others little more than a distorted reflection of our own narrow interests. In the *Diamond Sutra* the Buddha teaches that to become enlightened, we must purify our intentions. The core of consciousness must be purified before the content and structure of it can become clear.

14 Ultimate Tranquility Beyond Lakshana

Then, after hearing this sutra and comprehending its deep meaning,

Subhuti wept out loud and said to the Buddha, "Rare One,

World-honored One, of all the wise things[78] that I have ever heard, I

have never heard anything as profound as the sutra[79] that the Buddha

has just spoken. World-honored One, if anyone should hear this sutra

and believe it with a pure mind, then he will give rise to the true

lakshana,[80] and he will attain supreme goodness of the rarest kind.

World-honored One, the true lakshana is not a lakshana, and that is

why the Tathagata has called it a true lakshana.

"World-honored One, today I have heard this sutra, believed it,

understood it, received it, and upheld it, and this was not difficult.

If five hundred years from now, someone should hear this sutra, believe

it, understand it, receive it, and uphold it, then that person will be

a rare person indeed. And why is this? That person will be without

lakshana of self, lakshana of human beings, lakshana of sentient beings,

or lakshana of a soul. And why is this? Lakshana of self are not

lakshana, and lakshana of human beings, sentient beings, or souls are
not lakshana. And why is this? That which is disentangled from all
lakshana is called 'all buddhas.'"[81]

The Buddha said to Subhuti, "Just so, just so. Moreover, if a person
hears this sutra and does not become alarmed, or frightened, or scared,
then this person is indeed a rare person. And why is this? Subhuti, the
Tathagata has said that the supreme paramita[82] *is not the supreme*
paramita, and that this is what is called the supreme paramita
Subhuti, the Tathagata has said that the paramita of patience under
insult is not the paramita of patience under insult. And why is this?
Subhuti, long ago when my body was being cut apart by Kalingaraja,
I had no lakshana of a self, no lakshana of human beings, no lakshana
of sentient beings, and no lakshana of a soul. And why was this? If
at that distant time, as my body was being cut apart piece by piece,
if I had had lakshana of self, lakshana of human beings, lakshana of
sentient beings, or lakshana of a soul, I would have become angry. Sub-
huti, think about this some more; five hundred generations ago when
I was patient under insult, I was without lakshana of self, lakshana of
human beings, lakshana of sentient beings, or lakshana of a soul. For
this reason, Subhuti, a bodhisattva should disentangle himself from all
lakshana, and commit himself to highest complete enlightenment; and
he should not give rise to a mind based on form, and he should not give
rise to a mind based on sound, smell, taste, touch, or thought.

He should give rise to a mind that is not based on anything. Even if the

mind is based on something, it is not really based on anything, and for

this reason the Buddha says that the generosity of a bodhisattva should

not be based on form. Subhuti, a bodhisattva should be generous in

this way for the purpose of aiding all sentient beings. The Tathagata

says that all lakshana are not lakshana, and therefore he also says that

all sentient beings are not sentient beings.

"Subhuti, the Tathagata is one of real words, truthful words, correct

words, not false words, and not one who changes his words.[83] *Subhuti, the*

Dharma that the Tathagata has attained is not true and it is not false.

"Subhuti, when a bodhisattva bases his mind on some dharma and

then acts generously, he is like a person who has entered into dark-

ness—he sees nothing at all. But when a bodhisattva does not base his

mind on any dharma and then acts generously, he is like someone who

has eyes in the full light of the sun—he sees all forms clearly.

"Subhuti, if in future generations there are good men and good

women who can practice this sutra, and read it, and chant it, then the

Tathagata in his buddha wisdom will intimately know and intimately

see those people, and they will attain complete, limitless, and boundless

goodness."

This section is both very beautiful and very human. Subhuti is so
moved by the Buddha's words that he weeps. For his part, the Buddha

gives a personal account of his own past and the practices that led to his enlightenment. Reading it, one cannot help but realize again that the Buddha is speaking to human beings about human life. A buddha is a human being who has realized that he is a buddha; a human being is a buddha who has not yet realized that he is one. Subhuti's tears illustrate that enlightenment is not some cold abstraction, but an illumination and deepening of everything that comprises a human being. The Tathagata does not gaze upon us with a distant and antiseptic clarity, but with full realization of all of our thoughts and all of our intentions. He "sees and knows us intimately."

In this section, the Buddha speaks directly to Subhuti about some very human themes, and in so doing, he clears up any possibility of mistaking that the *Diamond Sutra* is a sutra of philosophical abstractions that have no bearing on the lives of real people. The Buddha's emphasis on life-as-it-actually-is is unmistakable when he swears that he is "one of real words, truthful words, correct words, not false words, and not one who changes his words." His description of his own past also leaves no doubt that this sutra is something to be practiced and used. These emphatic, personal, dramatic elements of the *Diamond Sutra* illustrate that the "Dharma that is not the Dharma" is not a Dharma that should be ignored or left unused. This is not mere philosophy; this is real life.

The *Diamond Sutra* addresses the concerns of the artist, the thinker, and the spiritual seeker. Like an artist, the Buddha shows us what he means by using examples from his own life and by illustrating his points with his own behavior. Like a thinker, he leads us to the very core of our awareness. And like a spiritual seeker, he shows us how to transcend the suffering of this world with a clear and specific practice. Even if one does not think of oneself as an artist, philosopher, or spiritual seeker, one cannot deny the *Diamond Sutra's* poetic power, its profound truths, and the perfection of the spiritual path it offers. Clearly the Buddha meant this sutra to be a spiritual teaching. In it he reveals the ultimate path to liberation; and yet as we read the Buddha's words, we become aware that this sutra is also a consummate work of philosophy and art. As an ultimate teaching, it brings together all of life's deepest concerns.

TRUE LAKSHANA

In Buddhist literature, the word *lakshana* usually refers to deluded awareness. "True lakshana," however, refers to ultimate truth and is a synonym for enlightenment. True lakshana is what a buddha sees.

Master Ching K'ung said, "The basic teaching of all Mahayana sutras concerns the true lakshana of all dharmas...Language can explain the true lakshana and allow us to contemplate it. By contemplating what it is, we cause it to become fully revealed. When it has become fully revealed, we will have become enlightened." He also says, "Highest complete enlightenment is the true lakshana of prajna. When one is beyond the grip of all lakshana and one practices all good dharmas, then one can contemplate prajna; and by this contemplation one can attain the true lakshana."

Chiang Wei-nung said that the heart of the *Diamond Sutra* lies in understanding true lakshana. Master Chih Yi said that the essential purpose of the *Diamond Sutra* is to teach people how to "use the wisdom of true lakshana to practice generosity without lakshana."

"True lakshana" is a name for the enlightened vision of a buddha. It is the highest and purest level of prajna. A buddha can describe true lakshana with words, but the rest of us must contemplate his description before we will be able to see it. True lakshana cannot be comprehended by the phenomenal mind.

NOT BECOME ALARMED, OR FRIGHTENED, OR SCARED

Ultimate prajna teachings can be very unsettling for some people. Buddhists are sometimes counseled not to teach these truths to people who might be frightened by them, because their fear may cause them to reject the Dharma.

Explications of the Wise One says that this line—"does not become alarmed, or frightened, or scared"—means: "When one first hears this sutra, one is not alarmed. Later, when one thinks about it, one does not become frightened. And lastly, when one practices it, one does not become scared."

The *Treatise of T'ien Ch'in* says, "'Alarmed' denotes that one does not believe that this sutra teaches the truth. 'Frightened' means that one is unable to overcome one's doubts about the Dharma. 'Scared' means that because of these two conditions, one is unable to practice this sutra."

PATIENCE UNDER INSULT

This virtue might also be called "patience under humiliation." The most difficult form of patience is patience under humiliation or insult. If one can bear this, one can bear anything. Usually this paramita is simply called the "paramita of patience." Patience under insult is a companion to generosity; both of these virtues are fundamental to the bodhisattva vow. Generosity is the most basic urge to reach out to others, while patience under insult is the most basic restraint needed when dealing with others. This is the reason that these two paramitas are highlighted in this sutra.

INTIMATELY KNOW AND SEE

Buddhists often describe our relationship with the Tathagata as involving feedback or "mutual interacting." As we look to the Tathagata, the Tathagata looks to us. As we strive to be good, our understanding of goodness is flooded with the Tathagata's understanding. If we practice this sutra, the Tathagata will know and see us. The *Awakening of Faith in the Mahayana* says that the Tathagata helps us most by being a brilliant example of perfect awareness that illuminates the darkness of our minds. Once glimpsed, we will never be able to take our eyes off its brilliance again. This is why as few as four verses of this sutra can lead us to enlightenment. Once mutual interaction has begun, there is nothing that can stop it, except the most profound forms of ignorance.

15 The Goodness of Upholding This Sutra

"Subhuti, even if a good man or a good woman were generous in the

morning with as many bodies as[84] *there are grains of sand in the Gan-*

ges River, and even if this generosity were repeated at midday with as

many bodies as there are grains of sand in the Ganges River, and even

if this generosity were repeated at night with as many bodies as there

are grains of sand in the Ganges River, and even if all of this gener-

osity were continued for an immense number of eons,[85] *still his or her*

goodness would not be as great as that of another person who heard

this sutra, who believed it, and who did not go against it. And if this

is so, imagine how much greater is the goodness of one who copies this

sutra, practices it, reads it, chants it, and explains it to others.

Subhuti, the most important thing that can be said about this sutra

is that its goodness is inconceivable, immeasurable, and boundless.

The Tathagata speaks this sutra to those who have committed

themselves to the great vehicle, he speaks it to those who have

committed themselves to the supreme vehicle.[86] *Those who uphold*[87] *this sutra, and read it, and chant it, and explain it to others, will be*

intimately known and intimately seen by the Tathagata. And all

such people will attain to a goodness that is immeasurable, unlimited,

boundless, and inconceivable. And all such people will share in the

highest complete enlightenment of the Tathagata. And why is this?

Subhuti, those who delight in lower dharmas cling to a view of a self,

a view of human beings, a view of sentient beings, and a view of a

soul, and thus they are not able to listen to this sutra, to receive it, to

read it, to chant it, or to explain it to others. Subhuti, in whatever

place this sutra can be found, it should be honored by all who are in

this world, and all in heaven, and all ashuras, and they should treat

this place as if it were a shrine; and they should surround it, and

bow to it, and pay their deepest respects to it. And they should scatter

incense and flowers all around this place."

The meaning of the *Diamond Sutra* intensifies as it spirals inward. The Buddha adds emphasis and specificity with each new section. The importance of sharing is reiterated and deepened in this part; the goodness of one who "upholds, reads, chants, and explains this sutra to others" is now "immeasurable, unlimited, boundless, and inconceivable." Upholding and sharing the *Diamond Sutra* is so important because this sutra establishes the basis for perfect compassion; prajna wisdom coupled with the sharing of that wisdom constitute the perfect foundation for all acts of compassion. When we are wise, we are not gripped by false attachments to form; when we are generous, we partake of those core intentions that are wisdom itself. Wisdom without compassion is not wisdom; the life of

Shakyamuni Buddha illustrates this point better than any simile or story could hope to do. The first section of the *Diamond Sutra* is a microcosm of the Buddha's life and an illustration of his compassion. Though he was enlightened, the Buddha spent most of his days teaching others.

In the *Mahaparinirvana Sutra,* the Buddha says, "Compassion is truth, and it is not a delusion. If someone asks, 'What is the source of all good roots?,' the answer is 'compassion.'" A few lines later, he says, "Those who do good are true thinkers, and true thought is compassion.... Compassion is the Tathagata. Good people, compassion is the bodhi way. The bodhi way is the Tathagata, and the Tathagata is compassion.... Good people, compassion is the inconceivable realm of all buddhas, and the inconceivable realm of all buddhas is compassion. One who knows compassion is a Tathagata. Compassion is the buddha nature of all sentient beings."

Elsewhere in the *Mahaparinirvana Sutra,* the Buddha describes a "vast realm of equanimity," saying that this realm is the "ground of all great bodhisattvas." His description of this realm offers another insight into the essential merging of pure compassion with pure wisdom. The Buddha says, "Good people, it resembles the vastness of space. In this realm, greed does not arise toward agreeable forms, and aversion does not arise toward disagreeable forms. When a great bodhisattva dwells in this realm, he is like that; he is without attraction or aversion toward agreeable and disagreeable forms. Good people, it resembles the vastness of space; it is without duality, and yet it includes all things. When a great bodhisattva dwells in this realm, he is like that; he is immense, without dualism, and able to contain all things. For these reasons, it is called the vast realm of equanimity."

The meaning of the *Diamond Sutra* is beyond words, and the goodness of it is beyond anything that the mind can conceive of. To comprehend this sutra is to see, however briefly, through the eyes of a buddha.

In the *Lankavatara Sutra* the Buddha says, "All ordinary consciousness is based on the error of grasping at lakshana and choosing among them. This tendency binds people to delusion; and it binds them to trains of false thinking."

The *Maharatnakuta* says, "Great bodhisattvas feel compassion when they look upon sentient beings who dwell in falsity, delusion, and dreams. In the midst of impermanence, deluded sentient beings give rise to false thoughts of permanence. In the midst of suffering, they give rise to false thoughts of pleasure. In the midst of no-self, they give rise to false thoughts of a self. In the midst of impurity, they give rise to false thoughts of purity.... When the bodhisattva contemplates these things, he feels great compassion for all sentient beings and thinks, 'How sad, how sad! Sentient beings have lost so much through their numerous errors. I must speak to them of the wonderful Dharma so they can free themselves from their delusions.'"

Prajna is called the "mother of all buddhas" for two reasons: (1) because it is the source of enlightenment, and (2) because it is the source of compassion. Wisdom is both clear and kind, both conscious and concerned; it is both sure of itself and forgiving of others. The *Diamond Sutra* teaches us how to be a mother to all sentient beings. In the *Mahaparinirvana Sutra*, the Buddha says, "When a great bodhisattva is generous toward all sentient beings, he should be equal-minded toward them all as if all of them were his children, and he should feel sympathy toward all of them. He should be like a mother who delights in caring for her sick child. And when that child is cured of his disease, he should be like a mother who takes delight in her child's health and lets go of the things that cured him. He should be like a mother who, seeing that her child is grown, takes delight in his independence.... If one is deficient in the paramita of generosity, one cannot achieve highest complete enlightenment."

If the Buddha is our mother, the *Diamond Sutra* is his clearest and surest method for curing us of the disease of deluded consciousness. With it, he cures us, then he leaves us so that he may take delight in our independence. When the river of delusion has been crossed, the raft of the Dharma must be left behind. Once we have achieved our independence, however, we should not forget the example of the Buddha, who showed us the way. All he asks in return and all that prajna wisdom requires is that we share the secret of our liberation with others.

16 Purification of Karma

"Furthermore, Subhuti, if a good man or good woman is slighted or ridiculed by others for upholding, reading, or chanting this sutra, it is due to bad karma incurred in a former life. That bad karma should be the cause of the person falling into a lower realm,[88] *but in this life he is just being slighted and ridiculed. Eventually his bad karma from previous lives will be eradicated, and he will attain highest complete enlightenment.*

"Subhuti, I remember countless eons ago, when I was before Dipankara Buddha,[89] *I met, honored, and made offerings to all of the countless buddhas*[90] *in the universe without excepting a single one of them. If someone in the Dharma-declining age can practice, read, and chant this sutra, the goodness he will attain will be a hundred times— nay, a billion billion*[91] *times, nay, an incalculable number of times that cannot even be suggested by metaphors—greater than the goodness I attained for honoring all buddhas.*

"Subhuti, if I were to say completely how great is the goodness

attained by a good man or a good woman who practices, reads, and

chants this sutra in the Dharma declining age,[92] *there would be those*

whose minds would become crazy upon hearing this, and they would

form deep doubts[93] *and not believe it. Subhuti, it is enough to know*

that this sutra is inconceivably great, and that the rewards it offers are

also inconceivably great."

In this section, the Buddha mentions for the first time the difficulty a devotee of this sutra might encounter in the real world. As is characteristic of this sutra, the Buddha's discussion of the problem is concise and to the point. Since human beings are social beings, the most difficult thing for human beings to bear is ridicule, humiliation, and social condemnation. The Buddha tells Subhuti that one might find oneself "slighted or ridiculed by others" for upholding this sutra. This single difficulty is meant to stand for all possible difficulties that might be encountered by one who upholds the *Diamond Sutra*. Other possible difficulties might be such things as sickness, economic hardship, emotional agony, war, natural disasters, and so forth. Although the Buddha mentions such problems in other discourses, here he does not, because the *Diamond Sutra* is a distillation of his prajna teachings.

Although patience under insult or humiliation is a supreme virtue and is the highest form of patience, it is usually treated as a subcategory of the paramita of patience. However, in this sutra, the Buddha refers to "patience under insult" as the "paramita of patience under insult." In doing so, he indicates that he is talking about the virtues of a bodhisattva rather than those of an ordinary person. The *Samdhinirmochana Sutra* says that patience under humiliation should be understood in three basic ways: (1) as patience under humiliation inflicted by others, (2) as patience under the humiliation of natural suffering, and (3) as "Dharma patience," or patience that is capable of seeing the true nature and cause of one's humiliation.

Patience under humiliation is as necessary to the bodhisattva as generosity. Generosity and patience are two sides of the same coin. Generosity looks toward the good of others, while patience does not recoil from their evil. A spiritual life without these essential virtues is not possible. Because of their fundamental importance, the Buddha emphasizes these two virtues and uses them in the *Diamond Sutra* to represent all the other virtues. Just as all delusion can be broken down into three basic causes—greed, anger, and ignorance—so all virtue can be explained in terms of generosity, patience, and wisdom. Generosity is the opposite of greed. Patience is the opposite of anger. Wisdom is the opposite of ignorance. The excellence of the Buddha's teachings and the clarity of his explanations can be found wherever we turn. The fourth virtue is "receive and uphold," "practice these teachings." The Buddha emphasizes this point often in the *Diamond Sutra* because resistance is a powerful part of human nature. It is one thing to agree with the Buddha that lakshana are delusive or that patience is a virtue; it is another thing altogether to actually put these truths into practice.

Only positive intentions can overcome resistance to the truth. One might earnestly say, "If there were no Dharma, all sentient beings eventually would find their buddha nature without it." The error in this statement is that on the road to discovering that buddha nature, each and every sentient being would rediscover the Dharma. The Dharma is conscious knowledge of the truth. It teaches us how to be aware and what to be aware of. Without its truths, we will continue to bring suffering on ourselves. With its truths, we will gradually remove all suffering from our minds.

In this section the Buddha mentions that one might be "slighted or ridiculed by others" for practicing this sutra. In the following lines, he tells us the cause of being ridiculed, the cure for it, and the result of that cure. Being "slighted or ridiculed" can mean anything from simple insults to serious physical injury; from being ignored to being beaten. The Buddha says that the cause of such unpleasant treatment is karma from a past life. He says that the cure is to continue practicing the *Diamond Sutra*. The results of this cure are that "the karma from previous lives will be eradicated and one will attain highest complete enlightenment."

Not bad, especially considering the alternatives. If one reacts with anger to being slighted or ridiculed by others, one only succeeds in planting more karmic seeds of the exact same type; one only succeeds in furthering the cycle of suffering and delusion; one does nothing to free oneself from the ignorance and duality that underlie all suffering. We all face this choice. Even the Buddha himself had to practice patience under insult. Buddhist sutras mention six times that the Buddha had to endure insult or humiliation:

1. When Sundari shouted at him angrily.
2. When Chinamanavika pretended she was pregnant with his child and tried to embarrass him in front of a large crowd.
3. When Devadatta pushed a stone down a hill at him.
4. When his clan was destroyed, and he had a headache for three days.
5. When he had to eat horse feed.
6. When he asked for alms, but was given none.

Even the enlightened Buddha had some karma remaining from past lives and thus had to endure insult and humiliation. One of the great teachings of the *Diamond Sutra* is that "all lakshana are delusive." When first encountered, this teaching may seem to be highly abstract and philosophical. By now, however, it should be clear that it is also an extremely practical spiritual technique. The thought that "all lakshana are delusive" can and should be used to help us overcome all forms of suffering. Just as we must realize that in all acts of generosity there is really no giver, no gift, and no recipient of any gift, so we must also be prepared to realize in times of humiliation that there is no one insulting us, no insult, and no one being insulted.

Karma is purified through this realization and its implementation. The moment we "receive and uphold" these truths and practice them in our lives, we begin to purify our karma. There is always a way to improve our situation.

KARMA

All actions produce effects. Intentional acts produce karmic effects. The Buddha taught that all volitional acts create "seeds" that are stored in the alaya consciousness. When these seeds germinate and grow, they produce a fruit of the same species. Compassionate acts produce karmic rewards, while cruel acts produce karmic retribution. What goes around comes around.

The Buddha generally spoke about three basic kinds of karma: karma generated by acts of the body, by acts of speech, and by acts of the mind. He often said that most people generate much of their bad karma through acts of speech.

To understand karma, we must understand that it is caused by our intentions and nothing more. In the *Diamond Sutra*, the Buddha emphasizes generosity because acts of generosity are karmically the purest, and most perfect of all acts. Prajna depends on both intellectual understanding and good intentions.

The world that we see around us is a product of our karma. The Buddha says that "all lakshana are delusive" in part because they all depend on our karma, and our karma arises from our "having lakshana of self, lakshana of human beings, lakshana of sentient beings, and lakshana of a soul." The world we see around us is primarily the result of our clinging to a sense of self. The lakshana that we see are the perceptible elements of our karma.

The Northern version of the *Parinirvana Sutra* says, "The good and bad results (of our actions) follow us like a shadow.... When this life is over, though we may regret what we have done, there is no way to come back and do it over again."

17 Complete and Utter Selflessness

Then Subhuti asked the Buddha, "World-honored One, when good

men and good women commit themselves to highest complete

enlightenment, on what should they base themselves? And how should

they subdue their minds?"

The Buddha said to Subhuti, "When good men and good women

commit themselves to highest complete enlightenment, they should

give rise to a mind like this: [94] *'I should save all sentient beings, and*

as I save them, I should know that there really are no sentient beings

to be saved.' And why is this? If a bodhisattva has lakshana of self,

lakshana of human beings, lakshana of sentient beings, or lakshana

of a soul, then he is not a bodhisattva. And why is this? Subhuti, in

truth, there is no such dharma as committing to highest complete

enlightenment.

"Subhuti, what do you say? When the Tathagata was in the realm

of Dipankara Buddha, was there an attainable dharma [95] *'highest*

complete enlightenment' or not?"

"There was not, World-honored One. As far as I understand the meaning of what the Buddha has said, when the Buddha was in the realm of Dipankara Buddha, there was no attainable dharma 'highest complete enlightenment.'"

The Buddha said, "Just so, just so. Subhuti, in truth, there is no dharma 'highest complete enlightenment' for the Tathagata to attain. Subhuti, if the Tathagata had attained a dharma 'highest complete enlightenment', then Dipankara Buddha would never have told me, 'In the future you will attain buddhahood and be called Shakyamuni.' Since there is no attainable dharma 'highest complete enlightenment', Dipankara Buddha told me that I would become a buddha, saying, 'In the future you will attain buddhahood and be called Shakyamuni.' And why is this? The Tathagata is the essence of all dharmas.[96] Someone might say, 'The Tathagata has attained highest complete enlightenment,' but Subhuti, there really is no dharma 'highest complete enlightenment' for the Buddha to attain.[97] Subhuti, the highest complete enlightenment that the Tathagata has attained lies between these two[98] and is neither true nor false.

"For these reasons, the Tathagata says that all dharmas are the Buddhadharma.[99] Subhuti, that which is said to be all dharmas is not all dharmas, and that is why it is called all dharmas. Subhuti, it is the same as a person growing up."[100]

Subhuti said, "World-honored One, the Tathagata has said that *when a person grows up,*[101] *he has not grown up, and that this is what*

is meant by growing up."

"Subhuti, a bodhisattva is just like that, and if he should say,

'I should save all sentient beings,' then he is not a bodhisattva.[102]

And why is this? Subhuti, there is no dharma called 'bodhisattva,'

and for this reason the Buddha has said that all dharmas have no

self, no human being, no sentient being, and no soul. Subhuti, if a

bodhisattva should say, 'I make the buddha realm magnificent,' then

he is not a bodhisattva. And why is this? The Tathagata has said that

that which makes the buddha realm magnificent is not magnificent,

and that that is what is called magnificence. Subhuti, only after a

bodhisattva has fully understood the dharma of selflessness[103] *will the*

Tathagata say that he is a true bodhisattva."

In this section the Buddha summarizes and deepens what he has taught
up to this point. As we read the *Diamond Sutra*, it is important to
remember that the Buddha is always deepening what he says. He works
like a master sculptor who fashions his art by the patient removal of
unwanted materials. As we watch him work, our appreciation of his
skills can only grow. Even a poor understanding of the *Diamond Sutra*
should lead one to an immense admiration of the Buddha, both for
what he says and for the way he says it.

In the beginning of this section, Subhuti again asks the Buddha,
"World-honored One, when good men and good women commit
themselves to highest complete enlightenment, on what should they
base themselves? And how should they subdue their minds?" These
are the same questions that Subhuti asked at the beginning of the

sutra. The Buddha's answer, which is now definitive, has two parts: (1) "When good men or good women commit themselves to highest complete enlightenment, they should give rise to a mind like this: 'I should save all sentient beings,' and (2) 'as I save them, I should know that there really are no sentient beings to be saved.'"

The first part of his answer, concerning what must be done, rests on the Buddha's teachings on compassion and generosity, while the second part, concerning how the first part should be understood, rests on his prajna teachings. The order of his answer is important; prajna wisdom follows generosity in the same way that peace follows compassion, or joy follows trust.

THE GENEROSITY OF SAVING ALL SENTIENT BEINGS

The key to understanding the Buddhadharma is to understand that the Buddha was both philosophical and practical; he always placed equal emphasis on philosophical truths and the moral implementation of those truths. A mystic and a practitioner, the Buddha could see to the heart of the universe, and yet he walked, ate, and spoke just like other people do. His middle path is the razor's edge between ultimate and conventional realities. The Buddha reveals the breadth of his nature in an amazing passage in the *Mahaparinirvana Sutra* when he concludes an exalted explication of the meaning and purpose of generosity by utilizing some of the rawest and most graphic metaphors found in any of his discourses. He says, "The purpose of generosity is to aid all sentient beings, and to help them overcome their defilements. When practicing generosity toward all sentient beings, do not hold to the view that there is a giver, a gift, or a recipient of a gift. Good people, imagine someone who has fallen into the ocean and who saves himself only by holding onto a corpse; a great bodhisattva who follows these teachings and practices generosity is like that; his generosity is just like that corpse. Good people, imagine a person shut away in a deep prison; all of the doors are locked and there is no way out except through a small hole in the latrine; the person saves himself and escapes from prison by crawling through that small hole; a great bodhisattva who follows these teachings and practices generosity is just like that…. Good people, imagine a sick person who cures himself only by eating unclean food; a great bodhisattva who follows these teachings and practices generosity is just like that."

Greed, anger, and ignorance are the three poisons that bind us to delusion. Generosity, patience, and wisdom are the antidotes to these poisons. *The Diamond Sutra* provides these antidotes and shows us how to take them. However, the sutra is so concise that most people need further instructions to fully understand it. The *Diamond Sutra* is a prajna teaching. Prajna teachings are generally concerned with emptiness. In contrast to these teachings, the Buddha also gave a series of "buddha nature" teachings. It is worth nothing that the Buddha gave buddha nature teachings after he gave prajna teachings. While prajna teachings explain what things are not, buddha nature teachings explain what they are. Because prajna teachings attempt to describe a reality so huge no words can contain it, they are usually stated in the negative. Buddha nature teachings attempt to describe that reality in positive terms. These two types of teachings reinforce each other and ultimately point to the same truths. Neither is meant as a substitute for the other. Both are needed to understand the Buddhadharma.

The *Mahaparinirvana Sutra* is a buddha nature teaching. Its more positive explications of enlightened reality and generosity can help us understand the *Diamond Sutra* better. As we read the passages below from the *Mahaparinirvana Sutra* and appreciate their beauty, we should remember not to cling to them. Buddha nature teachings cannot be properly understood if the wisdom of the *Diamond Sutra* is not applied to them. "All lakshana are delusive. If you can see that all lakshana are not lakshana, then you will see the Tathagata." If this point is remembered, the passages below can only deepen our understanding of the *Diamond Sutra.*

The Buddha said, "Since their vision is obscured by their many defilements, sentient beings cannot see nirvana, and thus they say that it is not there. A bodhisattva cultivates his mind and overcomes his defilements by practicing morality, meditation, and wisdom; thus he sees nirvana and knows that it is an eternal dharma, and not just some phenomenon that appears and goes away. Good people, imagine a deep hole filled with jewels in the middle of a dark room. Though people may know that the jewels are there, they are not able to see them because it is so dark. If someone should come into the room with a bright light and shine it in the hole, then everyone would be able to see the jewels. The person with the light is like a wise person who sees the truth; yet after he has shown the jewels to others, he does not think to himself that they are just some phenomenon that appears and goes away. Nirvana is like this; it is always there and it is not just some phenomenon that appears and goes away. Since ordinary people obscure it with their defilements, they do not see it. The Tathagata uses the light of wisdom to show them what nirvana is and where it is.... Nirvana is eternal and it never changes. It can be seen only after one has improved oneself by practicing goodness through an illimitable number of eons. Good people, imagine that there is good water deep under ground, but almost nobody knows that it is there. If a wise person should show them how to dig for the water, they would be able to get it. Nirvana is like that water; it is there, but we must be shown how to dig for it. Imagine a blind person who cannot see the sun or the moon. If he is given good medicine, then he will be able to see; and yet the sun and moon that he sees are not just phenomena that appear and go away. Nirvana is like that; it has always been there and it is not just some phenomenon that appears and goes away. Good people, imagine a law breaker who is in shackles and chains; at last he is released and allowed to go home to his family where he sees his father and mother, and brothers and sisters, and wife and relatives; nirvana is like that....

"Good people, there are two kinds of causes. One is the kind that makes something, while the other is the kind that completes something. A potter's ropes and wheels are implements of the first kind of cause, while lamps and candles are implements of the second kind of cause since they bring light to dark areas. Good people, nirvana is not attained by the first kind of cause; it is only attained by the second kind of cause. The thirty-seven conditions leading to buddhahood and the six paramitas are causes that complete something.

"Good people, simple generosity is a cause of nirvana, but not a cause of great nirvana. Only the paramita of generosity is a cause of great nirvana.... Good people, when a great bodhisattva practices the universal way of great nirvana, he does not hear generosity, and he does not see generosity. He does not hear the paramita of generosity, and he does not see the paramita of generosity. He does not hear nirvana, and he does not see nirvana. He does not hear great nirvana, and he does not see great nirvana. When a great bodhisattva practices great nirvana, he knows and sees the Dharma realm, he understands that true lakshana are empty and without absolute being, and he knows that there is no absolute lakshana that results from the convergence of perception and awareness. He attains the undefiled state and the state of non-doing. And he knows that all lakshana are like delusions that constantly change.... When the bodhisattva attains this state, he will be completely without greed, anger, or ignorance, and will neither hear them nor see them. This is called the true and real state of a great bodhisattva. When a great bodhisattva learns to dwell peacefully in this state, then she will realize for herself what the paramita of generosity really is.

"This state is also the state of prajna wisdom; it is the state of the prajna paramita. It is nirvana. It is great nirvana. Good people, why have I said that simple generosity is not the paramita of generosity? If one gives something because one is asked for it, this is simple generosity, and this is not the paramita of generosity. However, if one gives out of concern for others and without being asked to do so, then this is the paramita of generosity. If one gives from time to time, then this is simple generosity. However if one makes a practice of giving all the time, then this is the paramita of generosity. If one gives something to someone and then regrets what one has done, this is simple generosity. However, if one gives something away and does not regret what one has done, this is the paramita of generosity. A great bodhisattva knows that all material things can be taken away by kings, robbers, floods, or fires and thus he gives them away himself with great joy; this is the paramita of generosity. If in giving, one expects some reward, then one is merely practicing simple generosity and not the paramita of generosity. Only giving without any expectation of a reward can be called the paramita of generosity....

"Good people, if a person is like someone who plants a tree in order to obtain shade and coolness from it, and to obtain flowers, fruits, and wood from it, then he is merely practicing simple generosity, and not the paramita of generosity. A great bodhisattva who is practicing great nirvana does not see a giver, a gift, or a recipient of a gift. And he does not wait for an advantageous time, and he does not look for rewards, and he does not look to avoid rewards, and he does not see a cause in his act, or a condition, or a result. And he does not see a doer, or a receiver. And he does not notice whether the quantity is large or small, or the quality pure or impure. And he does not look down on the recipient, on himself, or on what is given. He does not see an observer, and he does not see a non-observer. And he does not record what he has done or to whom he has given. He resides wholly and only within the great universal dharma of nirvana. He practices generosity solely to help all sentient beings, and he practices generosity solely to help them overcome their defilements. When he practices generosity, he does not see a giver, a gift, or a recipient of a gift."

The state of a great bodhisattva who dwells completely within the paramita of generosity is also "the state of prajna wisdom; it is the state of the prajna paramita. It is nirvana. It is great nirvana." Because the Buddha taught different things to different people at different times, the Dharma can sometimes seem very complex and confusing. At its core, however, it is always the same; true generosity is always true wisdom; "it is the state of the prajna paramita. It is nirvana. It is great nirvana."

THE EMPTINESS OF ALL SENTIENT BEINGS

If sentient beings are empty of self-nature, why is there any need to save them? Why should one delusion attempt to help another delusion understand that both of them are deluded? One reason is that truth is both universal and compassionate. The universality of truth leads everyone toward enlightenment, while its compassionate aspects inexorably inspire us to care about others. The perfect equanimity of a buddha is the perfect fruition of truth; it is the omnipresent awareness of the unity of all things. The emptiness of sentient beings can be seen from the point of view of delusion, but it can also be seen from the point of view of a buddha. From an enlightened point of view, emptiness is the openness and infinitude of being. There is nothing there to be saved, and there is nothing to be gained by trying to save anything, and yet truth is truth—the dark shadows of delusion and separation simply cannot remain within the enlightened consciousness of a buddha.

Master Ching K'ung said, "*Prajna* means having a profound and correct understanding of the true nature of all things. It is completely different from what is known in this world as intelligence. Prajna is the cure for basic ignorance; it overcomes the poison of ignorance."

Sun Chien-feng said that the emptiness of sentient beings is emphasized in this place to avoid the tendency of using the "commitment to highest complete enlightenment as a lakshana on which to base oneself."

COMMITTING TO HIGHEST COMPLETE ENLIGHTENMENT

"Subhuti, there is no such dharma as committing to highest complete enlightenment." This is the third part of the Buddha's answer to Subhuti's question: "When good men and good women commit themselves to highest complete enlightenment, on what should they base themselves? And how should they subdue their minds?"

Highest complete enlightenment is the state of a buddha, and the goal of all Buddhist practice. In this section, the Buddha makes it very clear that even enlightenment is empty of absolutes. He says, "There really is no dharma 'highest complete enlightenment' for the Buddha to attain."

If there is no such thing as highest complete enlightenment, why would anyone want to be a Buddhist? If even the Buddha himself says that his own goal is empty, how can anyone make any sense of anything? Much of the brilliance and beauty of Buddhism lies in the Buddha's ability to craft explanations that speak to different levels of the mind. In the *Diamond Sutra*, he describes the highest and most rarefied levels of prajna wisdom. In the *Mahaparinirvana Sutra*, he looks at these same levels in a more detailed way. Notice how direct and lively the following exchange is.

The Buddha is asked: "The Tathagata has said that there are no absolute lakshana and no absolute results, but this is a contradiction because the Tathagata has also said that if one hears a line or a verse from the *Mahaparinirvana Sutra*, then one absolutely will attain highest complete enlightenment. The Tathagata has said that there are no absolutes and no results; however, if one attains highest complete enlightenment, one has attained something that is the same as an absolute lakshana or the lakshana of a result. Why then do you say that there are no absolutes and no results?"

The Buddha's answer to this question is in conformance with the teachings of the *Diamond Sutra*, but he completes his answer with a metaphor that is fully as powerful as any image found in postmodern *film noir:* "The teachings of all buddhas contain neither absolute lakshana nor absolute results. They are like the image of a person reflected in the blade of a knife; if the blade is held vertically, the image appears elongated, while if it is held horizontally, the image appears widened."

IT IS NEITHER TRUE NOR FALSE

In the *Diamond Sutra*, the Buddha says, "The Tathagata is the essence of all dharmas. Someone might say, 'The Tathagata has attained highest complete enlightenment,' but Subhuti, there really is no dharma for the Buddha to attain. The highest complete enlightenment that the Tathagata has attained lies between these two and it is neither true nor false."

What does "lies between these two" mean? How is it "neither true nor false?" Highest complete enlightenment lies between being an attainable state and not being a state at all. To achieve highest complete enlightenment is to be changed completely; it is to understand "the essence of all dharmas." If you merely think that you have grasped it, it is false. If you have really attained it, it is true. Highest complete enlightenment is an unnamable state. It lies outside all terms, concepts, and dharmas. The teachings of the Buddha can tell us roughly how to achieve that state, but they can never say precisely what it is.

In the *Mahaparinirvana Sutra*, the Buddha says, "Good people, imagine a person who wants to invite a king to his house. He must make his home as clean as he can, and he must prepare many delicious foods, before he can expect the king to come and visit him. A bodhisattva is just like that person; if he wants to invite the king who turns the wheel of highest complete enlightenment to come to him, he must purify himself as much as he can before he can expect the king to actually come.... A great bodhisattva does not see lakshana of form, the conditions behind forms, the bodies of forms, the origins of forms, or the disintegration of forms. He does not see a single lakshana, distinctions among lakshana, a seer, the forms of lakshana, or the recipient of form. And how is he able to do this? He is able to do this because he fully understands causes and conditions. All dharmas are just like this; they are all the same as dharmas of form."

They are all "like a person growing up"; we can see that something is there, but we can never say exactly what it is, and even if we could, the person would be different in the very next moment of time.

BETWEEN THESE TWO

In this section, the Buddha says that the Tathagata lies between being "the essence of all dharmas" and the reality that there "is no dharma 'highest complete enlightenment' that the Tathagata has attained." Many commentators explain this line by referring to the three truths discussed in chapter ten—namely, phenomenal reality, its emptiness, and the union of these two.

Master P'u Wan said that ultimate truth is the union of these three truths, adding that it "is like three animals crossing a stream; though the water is the same, each of them is covered to a different level by it. It is like three birds flying in the sky; though they appear to fly at different distances from us, they leave no trace on the sky itself."

Chiang Wei-nung said, "It should be understood that 'supreme emptiness' means neither being attached to things nor discarding or eliminating them. It is important to understand this if one wants to study prajna wisdom."

Master Ching K'ung said, "The Buddha taught a spiritual practice that is based on helping all sentient beings. If a practitioner clings to emptiness, how can he possibly succeed in helping anybody? Thus prajna requires that we cling neither to the phenomenal world, nor its basic emptiness."

Chiang Wei-nung said, "Every line of this sutra is like peeling a fruit. It is not easy to understand.... The reader is constantly asked to contemplate perfect non-attachment to all lakshana.... At the same time, he is also asked to seek goodness through acts of generosity. At no time should he allow himself to fall wholly on either side of these two truths. The deep truth lies between these two." He also said, "Prajna lies in clinging neither to the phenomenal world, nor to emptiness. If you say that generosity need not be practiced (because everything is empty), then you are making the mistake of clinging to emptiness."

Sun Chien-feng said that section seventeen is the beginning of the second half of the *Diamond Sutra*: "The first half uses [the idea of] disentangling from lakshana to overcome attachment, while the second half uses [the idea of] disentangling from thought to overcome even the tendency toward attachment." He also said, "The first half elucidates the emptiness of all things to reveal the unconditioned truth of prajna wisdom.... The second half elucidates the presence of all things to reveal that prajna and the manifestations of prajna [all phenomena] are one."

18 One Body Sees All

"Subhuti, what do you say, does the Tathagata have eyes of flesh[104] *or not?"*

"Yes, World-honored One, the Tathagata has eyes of flesh."

"Subhuti, what do you say, does the Tathagata have

heavenly eyes[105] *or not?"*

"Yes, World-honored One, the Tathagata has heavenly eyes."

"Subhuti, what do you say, does the Tathagata have

wisdom eyes[106] *or not?"*

"Yes, World-honored One, the Tathagata has wisdom eyes."

"Subhuti, what do you say, does the Tathagata have

Dharma eyes[107] *or not?"*

"Yes, World-honored One, the Tathagata has Dharma eyes."

"Subhuti, what do you say, does the Tathagata have

buddha eyes[108] *or not?"*

"Yes, World-honored One, the Tathagata has buddha eyes."

"Subhuti, what do you say, has the Buddha said that the sand

in the Ganges River is sand or not?"[109]

"Yes, World-honored One, the Tathagata has said that it is sand."

"Subhuti, what do you say, if there were as many Ganges Rivers as there are grains of sand in the Ganges River, and if all of the sand of all of those rivers were added up, and if the number of buddha realms equaled the number of all of those grains of sand, would that be a lot?"

"It would be very much, World-honored One."

The Buddha said to Subhuti, "The Tathagata intimately knows each and every sentient being in all of those worlds. And how can this be? The Tathagata has said that all minds are not minds and that that is what is called mind. And why is this so? Subhuti, the mind of the past cannot be gotten hold of,[110] the mind of the present cannot be gotten hold of, and the mind of the future cannot be gotten hold of."

Prince Chao Ming's title for this section might also be rendered in reverse: "In one contemplation the great body of all things is perceived." There is little difference between these renditions; they both mean something like "all sees all." In this section, the Buddha reiterates the all-knowing aspect of the Tathagata. He says again that the Tathagata "intimately knows" each and every mind in the universe. The way he builds up to this statement repeats a pattern characteristic of the *Diamond Sutra*. The Buddha asks Subhuti a series of questions that emphasizes the Buddha's own physical and spiritual reality, while at the same time emphasizes the reality and infinitude of sentient life. Following this, he declares that he "intimately knows" all minds in the universe. Lastly, he says that "all minds are not minds" because there is nothing about any mind or any stage of mental activity that can be gotten hold of or "attained." Just as there is no attainable dharma "highest complete enlightenment," so there is no attainable dharma "mind." In this case, the word *mind* should be understood in a very broad sense to include all of the following: "mind," "consciousness," "awareness," "cognition," "thought," etc.

In section seventeen, the Buddha tells Subhuti how a person should subdue his mind and on what he should base himself. In this section, he continues to explore the meaning of the word *mind*. The "mind" of the Tathagata is nothing more than the fulfilled and ultimate potential of each and every mind in the universe. The Tathagata is the "essence of all dharmas." His enlightenment "lies between" conventional and ultimate realities. Since his enlightenment cannot be described in conventional terms, it is not "true." However, since it is real in an ultimate sense, it is not "false" either.

To grasp just the surface meaning of the *Diamond Sutra* can be very difficult; to comprehend the deeper significance of that meaning is harder still; to fully realize the whole of it is to become a buddha. As we read, we should remember that the *Diamond Sutra* is the teaching of a buddha who is teaching us how to become buddhas ourselves. This sutra is as famous as it is because many people have found liberation through its teaching. The Tathagata tells us exactly what to do.

In this section, he takes us through the most important levels of conscious reality. As he does this he illustrates two points very clearly: (1) each level of awareness is real in its own way, and (2) the Tathagata is present at each level. This world is a delusion or a dream not because it is not present or "real," but only because it is not ultimately real. Just as we have eyes, so the Tathagata has eyes. Just as we have awareness, so the Tathagata has awareness. Indeed, he is so fully aware, he has completely transcended all individuality. Reality is like a face reflected in the blade of a knife; its properties depend on the angle from which we view it. Ultimately, "all minds are not minds and this is what is meant by mind."

19 Universal Transformation Within the Dharma Realm

"Subhuti, what do you say? If a person gives away enough precious jewels to fill an entire great chiliocosm, will this cause him to attain immense goodness?"

"Just so, World-honored One. This will cause him to attain immense goodness."

"Subhuti, if there really were such a thing as goodness, the Tathagata would never speak about attaining immense goodness. It is only because there is no such thing as goodness that the Tathagata says that immense goodness can be attained."

In the *Diamond Sutra*, the Buddha explains reality to beings who are conscious. One might make the absurd but intriguing speculation that if he were explaining reality to things devoid of consciousness, then his explanation would be different. This speculation is intriguing because it forces us to think of why the Buddha spoke so much about consciousness and not about material things. It is absurd but useful because it forces us to realize that there is no subject more important for conscious beings than the nature of their awareness. All of the Buddhadharma is concerned with the most fundamental aspects of awareness. One aspect of primitive awareness is poor self-awareness and the tendency to see the "content" of awareness as something other than awareness itself. The Buddha smashes this view over and over in the *Diamond Sutra*. The essential "content" of awareness is awareness itself. Once the false dharmas and things that occupy the minds of most sentient beings are seen for what they are, the awesome vision of the buddha eye will appear. The Tathagata is the "essence of all dharmas," his awareness is everywhere.

Prince Chao Ming's title for this section suggests that as one begins to understand the depths of consciousness, one becomes lost to a universal transformation within the Dharma realm. One enters the state in which "all sees all." The Tathagata "intimately knows each and every sentient being in the universe" because he is all of them. As the Buddha teaches the *Diamond Sutra*, he is us speaking to ourselves and he is us listening.

IMMENSE GOODNESS

The Buddha concludes this section by saying, "Subhuti, if there really were such a thing as goodness, the Tathagata would never speak about attaining immense goodness. It is only because there is no such thing as goodness that the Tathagata says that immense goodness can be attained." Just as highest complete enlightenment is "neither true nor false," so goodness also lies between these two. As soon as you think that you have it, you have lost it. As soon as you believe that you know with certainty what it is, you can be sure that you have begun to reify it and misunderstand the essential absence of all absolute qualities within it. Just as the foundation of consciousness cannot be found in the contents of consciousness, but only within consciousness itself, so the essence of goodness can only be found within itself. Only "because there is no such thing as goodness," does the Tathagata say that "they will attain immense goodness."

This section recalls section sixteen in which the Buddha says, "Subhuti, if I were to say completely how great is the goodness attained by a good man or a good woman who upholds, reads, and chants this sutra in the Dharma-declining age, there would be those whose minds would become crazy upon hearing this, and they would form deep doubts and not believe it. Subhuti, it is enough to know that this sutra is inconceivably great, and that the rewards it offers are also inconceivably great."

Where else is there a great teacher who denies everything he has ever taught? The "Buddhadharma is not the Buddhadharma"; "there is no such thing as goodness"; "there really is no dharma 'highest complete enlightenment' for the Buddha to attain"; "all minds are not minds and that is what is called mind." The brilliance of the Buddha ultimately lies in his ability to make us understand what he is talking about.

In the *Mahaparinirvana Sutra*, he gives explicit directions on how to attain the "inconceivably great rewards" offered by the Dharma. He says that no one can achieve nirvana without practicing four essential dharmas. "And what are these four? The first is be close to good friends. The second is listen to the Dharma with all of your mind. The third is think deeply about the Dharma. The fourth is do what the Dharma teaches you to do."

"Good friends" are those friends who help us find the truth and discourage us from doing evil. As Buddhists, all of us should strive to be this kind of friend to others. Good friendships are most easily maintained when we frequently discuss the Dharma with each other. The path of true friendship is the path of the bodhisattva who feels compassion for all sentient life everywhere.

Elsewhere in the *Mahaparinirvana Sutra*, the Buddha explains more about what he means by "listening to the Dharma." He says, "All sentient beings can learn to disentangle themselves from evil by listening to the Dharma. By listening to the Dharma they will achieve perfect goodness. For these reasons, listening to the Dharma is an important cause of bringing them near to great nirvana. Good people, imagine a brilliant mirror that perfectly reflects each and every detail of the human face. The mirror of listening to the Dharma is just like that; if you hold it up to yourself, it will reflect back to you in perfect detail all the good and evil that is within you. For these reasons, listening to the Dharma is an important cause of bringing you near to great nirvana. Good people, imagine a person who knows of a pool full of treasures, but does not know the way to the pool. If another person tells him the way, and if he follows that person's words, then he will attain great wealth, immeasurable wealth. All sentient beings are just like that person; they want to get to a good place where they can attain the treasures of the Dharma, but they do not know how to get around the many obstacles that lie on the way to that good place. A bodhisattva is someone who tells them how to get around those obstacles. If they follow his directions, they will arrive at that good place and attain supreme, great nirvana. For these reasons, listening to the Dharma is an important cause of bringing you near to great nirvana. Good people, imagine a drunken elephant who is consumed by his own fury and wants only to kill and cause destruction. Then imagine that there is an elephant master who succeeds in catching hold of the elephant's head with a metal hook, thereby subduing it and bringing an end to all of its terrible fury. All sentient beings are like that elephant; in a drunken rage of greed, anger, and ignorance, they want only to bring harm and evil into the world. Bodhisattvas use the metal hook of the Dharma to stop them and subdue their evil minds. For these reasons, listening to the Dharma is an important cause of bringing you near to great nirvana."

It is good to see yourself as a drunken elephant consumed by your own furious greed, anger, and ignorance. And it is good to see yourself as a bodhisattva who subdues the beast and brings an end to all of its terrible rage. The most important way to "think deeply about the Dharma" is to apply its teachings to your own life. All of us know the urges of greed, anger, and ignorance; if you have read this far, you probably also know the great satisfaction that comes from subduing those urges. We become a good friend to others only after we have seen ourselves in the mirror of the Dharma.

The Buddha says that the fourth cause of attaining nirvana is doing "what the Dharma tells you to do." It is never enough just to listen to it or to rely on others to tell you what to do. In the passage above, the Buddha chooses his words very carefully; he says that "listening to the Dharma is an important cause of bringing you near to great nirvana." He does not say that listening alone will give you nirvana or even bring you to nirvana; he says that it will "bring you near to great nirvana." The rest you must do for yourself. The bodhisattva shows you the obstacles on your path, but it's up to you to walk around them. The Buddha gives you the medicine, but you have to take it.

In a later passage of the *Mahaparinirvana Sutra*, the Buddha makes this point explicit: "One does not attain great nirvana just by listening to the Dharma. To attain great nirvana, one must do what the Dharma says to do. Good people, imagine a sick person; he cannot be cured simply by hearing the name of a medicine that can cure his disease; he must take that medicine to be cured. In this same way, simply hearing about the Dharma is not enough to bring an end to your problems; you must think deeply about what you have heard [and put it into practice]. And how do you practice the Dharma? Practicing the Dharma means practicing all of the paramitas, from the paramita of generosity to the paramita of wisdom."

20 Beyond Form and Lakshana

"Subhuti, what do you say? Can the Buddha be seen in his complete form body[111] or not?"

"No, World-honored One, the Buddha ought not to be seen[112] in his form body. And why is this? The Tathagata has said that his complete form body is not the complete form body, and that this is what is called the complete form body."

"Subhuti, what do you say? Can the Tathagata be seen by means of all complete lakshana[113] or not?"

"No, World-honored One. The Tathagata ought not to be seen by means of all complete lakshana. And why is this? The Tathagata has said that the completeness of all lakshana[114] is not completeness and that this is what is called completeness of all lakshana."

The Tathagata is not a thing. This point should be clear by now. The Tathagata cannot be defined by anything because all possible terms of definition are less than the Tathagata. The Tathagata is neither a "him," nor a "her," nor an "it." Language uses patterns derived from the material world, and thus much of our thinking is unconsciously constrained by material imperatives. We tend to think in hard bits comprised of subject, verb, and object, and we tend to bind these bits into hardened sentences that must begin with a capital letter and end with a period. These grammatical conventions evolved from patterns that were first discovered and used by primitive human beings. For atomized, object-oriented communication and for dealing with categorizable thoughts, these conventional linguistic patterns work very well. They are good for some things, but not for everything. In some cases, they lead us to completely misunderstand the nature of our minds and the universe in which we live. Our tendencies to categorize, compartmentalize, and reify our world, can be our own worst enemy when we are trying to understand the ultimate teachings of the Buddhadharma.

Our tendencies to lock ourselves into limiting linguistic patterns are as strong today as they were in the Buddha's time. Much of the *Diamond Sutra* is intended to help us break free of limited thought patterns that are derived more from the movements of our bodies in the material world than from the essential elements of awareness itself. In the *Diamond Sutra*, the Buddha repeatedly smashes our tendency to imprison our minds within matter-oriented constructions. Lakshana are delusive the moment we reify them and treat them like hard and fast objects. Our sense of having a separate consciousness that is seated upon a separate self is based solely on our perceptions of having a body, which in a limited sense, and only in a limited sense, meets some of its needs in isolation. It is a mistake to believe that the whole of conscious life can be confined to this small and isolated circle of material considerations. And it is an error to believe that the universe can be contained within this circle.

The Buddha spent years challenging these errors and misperceptions, and yet there is a core of truth at the heart of these limiting mistakes. The mind is the measure of all things; it must only be turned in the right way. When the image we see in the knife blade is turned just so, our minds will give us information that leads to ultimate understanding of the universe and consciousness itself. In the *Diamond Sutra*, the Buddha shows us how to turn the blade and cut through our delusions.

21   Speaking the Unspeakable

"Subhuti, never say that the Tathagata has this thought: 'I have some Dharma to speak about.' Do not have that thought.[115] And why is this? If someone says that the Tathagata has a Dharma to speak about, then that person is defaming the Buddha, and he does not understand what I have been saying. Subhuti, one who speaks the Dharma has no Dharma to speak about and that is what is called speaking the Dharma."

Then the wise Subhuti[116] said to the Buddha, "World-honored One, will there ever be sentient beings in the future who upon hearing this Dharma will give rise to believing minds?"

The Buddha said, "Subhuti, those sentient beings are not sentient beings, and they are not not sentient beings.[117] And why is this? Subhuti, the Tathagata has said that all sentient beings are not sentient beings and that this is what is called sentient beings."

In this section the Buddha declares, "Subhuti, one who speaks the Dharma has no Dharma to speak about, and this is what is called speaking the Dharma." This denial of an absolute Dharma should be familiar by now. In these last sections, the Buddha's tone changes. In previous sections, he guided Subhuti with leading questions; now he instructs him in no uncertain terms. This section begins with the phrase, "Subhuti, never say..." By this section, the Tathagata has made his point; now he will remove all doubt about what he has said. The rhetorical pattern of the *Diamond Sutra* is one of the most basic and effective of all communication techniques; first, you say what you are going to say, then you say it, and then you say what you have said. At each turn in this process, the Buddha's reasoning cuts deeper as his tone grows more commanding. Interestingly, he does not answer Subhuti's question about belief with a statement about belief, but with the assertion that there are no sentient beings to believe or not believe. Just as the Buddha has no Dharma to speak about, so there are no sentient beings to hear it. This ultimate level of truth is difficult even to glimpse with the unenlightened mind.

The *Sutra of Complete Enlightenment* says, "To describe enlightenment, one must rely on the delusion of words, and thus one's description will be fundamentally delusional. Since one's description is delusional, the Dharma of which one has spoken must also be a delusion."

22 The Unattainable Dharma

Subhuti said to the Buddha, "World-honored One, is it not so

that when the Buddha attained highest complete enlightenment,

nothing was really attained?"

"Just so, just so. Subhuti, there is not even the slightest dharma

that can be attained in highest complete enlightenment,[118] *and this*

is what is called highest complete enlightenment."

This section repeats and thus emphasizes an earlier point. Subhuti's question allows the Buddha to make his point perfectly clear.

Hsiao Yao-weng said, "When one knows that one's body and mind are empty, and when one knows that everything outside one's body is empty, then one has broken the hold of all lakshana, and one very naturally ceases to cling to things or argue about them. This state is called the joy of Ch'an."

The *Dhammapada* says, "Go through the day seeing as if you were not seeing a thing. And go through the day hearing as if you were not hearing a thing."

Prajna is usually understood to have three levels. The first level resides in words; we learn the truth by reading or listening to words. The second level is discovered in contemplation; we deepen our understanding of what we have read or heard by contemplating it. The third level is actual experience of the truth. There are five basic contemplations that can help us experience prajna truth:

1. Contemplate that all phenomena, including the body and the psychological sense of having a separate self, arise from a combination of many factors and conditions. Deep down, all of these things are empty. None of them has a permanent or absolute nature of its own.
2. Contemplate that all things are interconnected and that all of them are part of one "great body."
3. Contemplate that all things ultimately reside in the perfect tranquility of nirvana.
4. Contemplate the absence of all phenomenal thought. If there are no phenomenal thoughts, there can be no delusions.
5. Contemplate the perfect equality of all things. This contemplation leads to mental equipoise and a profound awareness of the buddha within.

Kuei T'ai-ch'uan said, "Thoughts all start and stop in the mind. When thoughts arise, defilements arise; when thoughts stop, defilements cease. Thus, there is really nothing better than simply not thinking."

The ancients used to say, "When no thought arises, the whole world is clear. When the six senses move, the world is covered with clouds."

The *Awakening of Faith in the Mahayana* says, "All realms are the product of the movement of the deluded mind. If the mind does not move, then all realms and all lakshana will disappear. Only the true mind is universal and omnipresent."

23 Perfect Equanimity

"Furthermore, Subhuti, this dharma is equal and without

high or low; it is called highest complete enlightenment.

Highest complete enlightenment is attained by cultivating all

good dharmas[119] *while being without self, without human*

being, without sentient being, and without soul. Subhuti,

when I say 'all good dharmas,' the Tathagata is saying that not

all good dharmas is what is called all good dharmas."

Up until now, the Buddha has said only what highest complete enlightenment is not. In this section he says what it is. He says that it is "equal and without high or low," that it is attained by "cultivating all good dharmas," and that this cultivation must be done without the lakshana of "self, human being, sentient being, or soul."

In the *Mahaparinirvana Sutra*, the Buddha describes a state called "diamond samadhi." He says that when a great bodhisattva "rests in diamond samadhi he is able to overcome all dharmas and see that all of them are impermanent, the mere movements of lakshana. And he can see that there are no real causes for fear, illness, suffering, or victimization.... Dwelling in this samadhi, a bodhisattva is generous to sentient beings even as he knows that they are not ultimately real. And his practice of all of the paramitas—from the paramita of morality to the paramita of wisdom—is like this, for if a bodhisattva believes that there really are such things as sentient beings, then he cannot truly fulfill any of the paramitas.... Diamond samadhi contains all other samadhis.... When a great bodhisattva cultivates this samadhi, you should know that he is cultivating all other samadhis.... Good people, when a bodhisattva resides in diamond samadhi, he is able to see all dharmas without the slightest obstruction and is able to observe them all as clearly as he would an *amala* fruit held in the palm of his hand, and yet he never has the thought that he is 'seeing all dharmas.' ...Good people, diamond samadhi is like climbing to the top of a tall mountain that provides a clear view of everything around. Good people, it is like misting rain under a spring moon; the drops of water are very tiny and close together, and it takes someone with very clear vision to see the spaces between them. A bodhisattva who attains diamond samadhi is like that—his vision is exceptionally clear.... Good people, just as a diamond can cut through all other substances and yet never have the thought that it is cutting through anything, so diamond samadhi can cut through all defilements without ever having the thought that it is cutting through anything. Good people, it is like the earth, which can support all things without ever having the thought that it is support-ing anything; it is like fire that burns without ever thinking that it is burning anything, or like water that soaks things without ever thinking that it soaks anything; it is like the wind that never thinks that it can move things; it is like open space that never thinks that it can contain all things. Just as nirvana never gives rise to the thoughts or words—'I lead all sentient beings to tranquility'—so diamond samadhi, though it can overcome all suffering, never has the thought 'I can overcome all suffering.' If a bodhisattva can peacefully reside within this diamond samadhi, she can become a buddha in the space of a single thought."

24 True Generosity Lies in Upholding This Sutra

"Subhuti, if a person were to perform an act of generosity by

giving away a quantity of precious jewels equal to all of the

Sumeru mountains within a great chiliocosm; and if another

person were to uphold as few as four verses of this

Prajnaparamita Sutra, and read them, and chant them,

and explain them to others, the goodness of this second person

would be a hundred times—nay, a billion billion[120] times,

nay, an incalculable number of times that cannot even be

suggested by metaphors—greater than the goodness of the

first person."

This section prevents anyone from misunderstanding either what the "good dharmas" that lead to the attainment of highest complete enlightenment really are, or how they should be understood. Consciousness and conscious meaning that turn and reflect upon themselves may appear to be trapped in circular reasoning, and yet, nothing could be further from the truth. Consciousness that discovers itself within itself rises in a spiral of wisdom; at each turn, more of what is false is left behind.

The *Sutra of Perfect Enlightenment* says, "Ignorance has no basis whatso-ever in reality. It is like a dream; while we are dreaming, our dreams seem to be real, but as soon as we awaken, we can see that nothing was there."

25   Transforming That Which Cannot Be Transformed

"Subhuti, what do you say? Don't any of you ever say that the Tathagata has this thought: 'I am saving sentient beings.' Subhuti, don't have this thought. And why is this? In truth, there are no sentient beings for the Tathagata to save. If there were sentient beings for the Tathagata to save, then the Tathagata would have lakshana of self, human being, sentient being, and soul.

"Subhuti, when the Tathagata speaks of a self, it is the same as no self, and yet all ordinary people take it as a self. Subhuti, the Tathagata says that ordinary people are not ordinary people, and that this is what is called ordinary people."

The beginning of this section contains one of the only phrases in the *Diamond Sutra* that seems to be out of place: The Buddha says, "Subhuti, what do you say? Don't any of you ever say that..." The Buddha begins with a question, and then immediately makes a declaration. Subhuti never answers his question. It would seem that the oft-repeated phrase "what do you say" does not quite belong here. Rather than reading something into this, it is probably best to leave it with a small question mark. This small anomaly does not change the meaning of the passage at all.

As he delivers the teachings of this sutra, the Buddha is speaking to all of the monks present, and yet up until this point, he mainly directs his comments to Subhuti. This section of the *Diamond Sutra* contains the second line spoken by the Buddha that verbally acknowledges his entire audience (the first occurs at the end of section six). He says, "don't any of you ever say that..." The tone is unmistakably that of a teacher who has explained his subject and who now wants to be sure that it sinks in and is applied correctly. The whole of the *Diamond Sutra* is addressed to anyone who is fortunate enough to hear it or read it. In these concluding sections, the Buddha clears away all doubt about what he means. It is good to remember that Prince Chao Ming's division of the sutra into thirty-two sections is something that was brought to it later; the actual sutra was a continuous discourse that takes about forty minutes to read out loud. Though we have no way of knowing how long the Buddha actually took to give this teaching or whether he paused to emphasize his points, it is hard not to imagine him looking directly at his monks and watching their responses as he says, "Don't any of you ever say that the Tathagata..."

26 The Dharma Body Is Without Lakshana

"Subhuti, what do you say? Can the Tathagata be seen by his thirty-two marks or not?"

Subhuti said, "Just so, just so.[121] The Tathagata can be seen by his thirty-two marks."

The Buddha said, "Subhuti, if the Tathagata could be seen by his thirty-two marks, then a wheel-turning sage-king[122] would be the same as the Tathagata."

Subhuti said to the Buddha, "World-honored One, as far as I understand the meaning of what the Buddha has said, one ought not to be able to see the Tathagata by his thirty-two marks."

Then the Buddha spoke a verse:

> *If anyone should think that I can be seen among forms,*
>
> *Or that I can be sought among sounds,*
>
> *Then that person is on the wrong path*
>
> *And he will not see the Tathagata.*

In this section, the Buddha clears up one of the last remaining ways that this sutra could be misunderstood. He asks Subhuti if the Tathagata can be seen by the thirty-two marks of a Buddha. Subhuti mistakenly says, "Just so, just so. The Tathagata can be seen by his thirty-two marks." The Chinese word used for "see" (*kuan*) here is slightly different from the word that has been used all along (*chien*), but this change only strengthens the Buddha's correction of Subhuti's mistake. Kuan means to observe or to contemplate, while chien is roughly the same as the English words "look" or "see." In this case, kuan also means "to see." Whatever verb is used, the core idea remains the same—the Tathagata cannot be grasped, contained, viewed, contemplated, seen, or defined by any lakshana or any combination of lakshana, no matter how perfect or complete they are.

The Buddha says, "Subhuti, if the Tathagata could be seen by his thirty-two marks, then a wheel-turning sage-king would be the same as the Tathagata." The thirty-two marks of a Buddha are discussed below. Before we get to that point, though, it should be emphasized that the deep meaning of this passage is not concerned with these marks. It is concerned only with denying one of the last possible ways that someone might mistake the Buddha's overall point—that "all lakshana are delusive," that none of them is essentially real. The Tathagata cannot be understood in terms of any possible lakshana, including those of his *sambhogakaya.*

The *Avatamsaka Sutra* says, "If you do not understand the true nature of things, then you will not see the Buddha."

THE THIRTY-TWO MARKS OF A BUDDHA

It is surely no accident that Prince Chao Ming chose to divide this sutra into thirty-two parts, for this is the same number of marks that identify a buddha's sambhogakaya—a buddha's "reward body." It can only be perceived by highly advanced bodhisattvas or other buddhas. All buddhas have three bodies: a *nirmanakaya*, a *sambhogakaya*, and a *dharmakaya.* Buddhas appear before ordinary sentient beings in their nirmanakaya, or "transformation bodies." They achieve perfect unity with everything in the universe and beyond in the dharmakaya, or "dharma body." They condition the realms over which they preside in their sambhogakaya. A buddha's sambhogakaya is a manifestation of his perfected intentions. The sambhogakaya of all buddhas have thirty-two distinctive marks, or lakshana. These marks are a result of a buddha's behaviors before becoming enlightened and a symbol, or signifier, of those behaviors after becoming enlightened. Wheel-turning sage-kings also possess the thirty-two marks.

The *Treatise on the Perfection of Great Wisdom* describes the thirty-two marks of a buddha's sambhogakaya as follows:

1. The bottoms of the feet are flat and soft so that they come into perfect contact with the ground. This signifies the perfect path that the buddha walked before he became a buddha as well as his ability to lead others on that same path.

2. There is a mandala at the bottom of each foot. These mandalas have the power to defeat or overcome all enemies and all evil demons. They signify the Buddha's ability to overcome all forms of ignorance. Some sources say that these mandalas also appear on the Buddha's hands.

3. His fingers and toes are long, straight, and well-formed. This sign arises because the Buddha was never proud, and because he always showed reverence and respect for his teachers. It signifies his ability to lead sentient beings to the truth.

4. The heel of the foot is large and flat because he was moral, listened to the Dharma, and practiced it with great diligence. It signifies his ability to transform others by his example.

5. His fingers and toes are webbed. This mark arises from his exemplary practice. It signifies his absence of all defilement.

6. His hands and feet are soft. This is a result of his having used his hands to care for the ill. This signifies his gentleness and compassion.

7. The top of his foot is high and well-formed due to his constant application of effort. It signifies the benefit and strength that he can bring to the service of all sentient beings.

8. His thighs and buttocks are well-formed due to the attentiveness with which he listened to the Dharma and preached it. This signifies that all his bad karma has been eradicated.

9. While his arms are hanging at his sides, his fingers reach below his knees. This mark signifies generosity and an absence of pride and greed. It also shows that he is capable of defeating any demon that may attack him.

10. His penis is concealed within his body due to his fearlessness and lack of sensual lust. It signifies a long life and many disciples.

11. His body is tall and large like a full grown banyan tree. This is a result of his having preached the Dharma and taught fearlessness for many ages. It signifies that he is a supreme teacher.

12. All the hair on his head and body curls gently to the right, and all of it is light blue and soft. This mark is a result of his having achieved all good dharmas. It signifies his ability to lead sentient beings and cause them to feel joy through his good example.

13. Fine body hairs the color of lapis lazuli grow from every pore in his body. Each of these pores also emits a wonderful fragrance. This mark results from his respect for all sentient beings, and his constant effort to teach them strength, tirelessness, and diligence.

14. His skin is the color of gold due to his compassion and his complete lack of anger. This mark signifies his ability to teach non-attachment and goodness.

15. His body emits a light that permeates the universe. This light is a result of his compassionate vows. It signifies his ability to overcome all obstacles and attain all good dharmas.

16. His skin is soft and supple, and dust does not cling to it. This mark arises from his purity and wisdom. It signifies his even-mindedness and his ability to help all sentient beings achieve enlightenment.

17. His hands, feet, shoulders, and neck are soft, large, and well-formed due to his generosity. This signifies his ability to help all sentient beings overcome their defilements.

18. His sides are large and well-formed. This mark arises from the care he gave to others. It signifies his ability to cure sentient beings of illness and satisfy all their needs.

19. His upper body is as large and powerful as a lion. This is a result of his lack of pride and deceit. It signifies his immense tolerance and compassion.

20. His body is very large. This mark arises from the help he has given to others. It signifies his ability to end suffering and teach others right thoughts.

21. His shoulders are broad and even. This mark arises from the shrines he built and from the many times he taught others not to be afraid. It signifies his ability to overcome all defilements.

22. He has forty teeth, all of which are even and white as snow. This mark arises from his perfect speech. It signifies his ability to teach sentient beings how to overcome all verbal and emotional defilements.

23. His teeth are neither too big nor too small, and the spaces between them are narrow. There are no large gaps between his teeth. This mark arises from the good dharmas he uses to help others. It signifies his ability to empathize with others and lead them by first understanding them.

24. His teeth are white, sharp, and hard. This mark arises from his contemplation of all good dharmas, and his cultivation of compassion. It signifies his ability to help sentient beings overcome the stubborn defilements of greed, anger, and ignorance.

25. His cheeks are full and strong like a lion's. Anyone who sees this mark will eradicate the bad karma of hundred eons and attain a vision of all buddhas.

26. His mouth tastes only the best flavors. This mark arises from his seeing all sentient beings as his own children. It signifies the perfection of his teachings and the Dharma's ability to lead everyone to enlightenment.

27. His tongue is wide and long. This mark arises from his compassionate vows. Anyone who sees it will eradicate eons of bad karma.

28. His voice is as beautiful as a heavenly instrument due to his practice of always praising others and being honest. Those who hear his voice will be filled with as many good dharmas as they are capable of receiving.

29. His eyes are as blue as blue lotus flowers. This mark arises from his always seeing others in a compassionate light and the joy he feels in helping them.

30. His eyelashes are fine and perfectly arranged. This mark arises from his serving all sentient beings as if they were his parents.

31. There is a fleshy mass on the top of his head. This mark arises from his teaching others the ten good dharmas.

32. There is soft, white hair between his eyes. The hair curls to the right and emits light. This mark arises from his exhorting sentient beings to practice the three trainings: morality, meditation, and wisdom. It is a good meditation technique to try to see this light.

27 Nothing Is Ended
and Nothing Is Extinguished

"Subhuti, consider this thought: [123] *'the Tathagata attains highest*

complete enlightenment because his lakshana [124] *are incomplete.'* [125]

Subhuti, do not have this thought: 'the Tathagata attains highest

complete enlightenment because his lakshana are incomplete.'

   "Subhuti, consider this thought: 'the one who commits to high-

est complete enlightenment [126] *says that all dharmas are ended and*

extinguished.' [127] *Do not have this thought. And why is this? The*

one who commits to highest complete enlightenment does not say

that lakshana are ended and extinguished among dharmas." [128]

In section twenty, Subhuti and the Buddha have the following exchange:
"Subhuti, what do you say? Can the Tathagata be seen by means of all
complete lakshana or not?"

   "No, World-honored One. The Tathagata ought not to be seen by
means of all complete lakshana. And why is this? The Tathagata has
said that the completeness of all lakshana is not completeness and that
this is what is called completeness of all lakshana."

"Completeness" of lakshana connotes a best possible case; it means that even if the combination of lakshana is perfect, the Tathagata still cannot be seen by means of it. In this section, the Buddha addresses a way that this claim might possibly be misunderstood. In keeping with the last part of the *Diamond Sutra*, his tone is more authoritative and commanding than before. Rather than lead Subhuti toward the right conclusion with a series of questions, the Buddha simply tells him: "Subhuti, do not have this thought: 'the Tathagata attains highest complete enlightenment because his lakshana are incomplete.'" It is not incompleteness or any kind of imperfection that leads to highest complete enlightenment. The point made in section twenty that the "Tathagata ought not to be seen by means of all complete lakshana" means that he cannot be seen by any lakshana or any combination of lakshana. It does not mean that he is the Tathagata because he some-how lacks completeness of form, or completeness of lakshana.

It also does not mean that he is the Tathagata because he has "ended" or "extinguished" some or all of "his" lakshana. The *Diamond Sutra* teaches the emptiness of lakshana, not their extinction.

Master Tan Hsu (1875–1963) said that the *Diamond Sutra*, in general, teaches four main points: (1) the way to become free from all karma by going beyond all lakshana, (2) the way to overcome defilements by being both unattached to all things and completely aware of the depths of prajna wisdom, (3) the way to end all suffering by understanding the true nature of the dharma body, and (4) the way to overcome the delu-sions of past, present, and future by committing to highest complete enlightenment.

28 Not Receiving and Not Wanting to Receive

"Subhuti, if one bodhisattva gives away enough precious jewels to fill
as many worlds as there are grains of sand in the Ganges River, and
if a second knows that all dharmas are without self [129] *and thus attains*
patience, then the goodness attained by the second bodhisattva is
superior to the first bodhisattva. Subhuti, this is because all bodhisattvas
do not receive goodness." [130]

Subhuti said to the Buddha, "World-honored One, why do you
say that bodhisattvas do not receive goodness?"

"Subhuti, bodhisattvas should not be greedy or attached to the
goodness that they do; this is why I say that they do not receive goodness."

This section completes the Buddha's explanation of generosity,
patience, and goodness. It is no accident that the Buddha mentions the
principal virtues of a bodhisattva immediately after having talked about
"one who commits to highest complete enlightenment." His message
that ultimate wisdom must include compassion should be clear by now.

The *Avatamsaka Sutra* says, "Supreme enlightenment does not come
from somewhere and it does not go somewhere; its pure and wondrous
being is revealed only in spirit."

29 Awesome Tranquility

"Subhuti, if someone says, 'It seems as if the Tathagata comes and goes, and sits and lies down,' then this person has not understood my meaning. And why is this? The one who is the Tathagata has not come from somewhere, and he is not going somewhere, and that is why he is called the Tathagata."

If one has followed the *Diamond Sutra* with care, this chapter says it all. The Buddha's evocation of his corporal form, followed by his denial of that form, is very moving.

The Buddha says, "The Tathagata has not come from somewhere, and he is not going somewhere" because the Tathagata always is. The consciousness that is the Tathagata not only transcends all duality, but also all time, all phenomenal form, all lakshana, and all conceptualization. Tathagata means "thus come one," but he cannot be perceived as a mere body that "comes and goes." The Buddha makes certain that we understand this by saying "Subhuti, if someone says, 'It seems as if the Tathagata comes and goes, and sits and lies down,' then this person has not understood my meaning." The body of the Buddha that can be perceived within phenomenal reality is called his *nirmanakaya* or "transformation body." It is a body that exists dependent on phenomenal conditions, and as such, it is born, grows old, and dies, just as all phe-nomenal bodies do. This body is also called the body of the Buddha's "transformed nirvana," because the karma of the people living in India at that time was right for his nirvana to "transform" into a physical form. Though those of us who are alive today do not have the karma to see the Buddha's transformation body, we do have the karma to hear his message and learn from it. Though we may feel sad that we cannot see the Buddha's transformation body, we can be sure that following his teachings will lead us to discover the fullness of his consciousness as it resides within our own minds.

Ch'an Master Ju Man (early ninth century) said, "The Buddha comes from the unconditioned and returns to the unconditioned.... He comes for sentient beings and leaves for sentient beings. The pure sea of the bhutatathata is everlasting, deep, and clear. The wise think often of this and do not become perturbed."

30 Compound Lakshana

"Subhuti, if a good man or a good woman were to pulverize a great

chiliocosm into fine dust, what do you say, would that collection

of fine dust [131] be a lot or not?"

"It would be a lot, World-honored One. And why is this? If that

collection of fine dust were something that really existed, the Buddha

would not have called it a collection of fine dust. And why is this?

The Buddha has said that a collection of fine dust is not a collection

of fine dust and so it is called a collection of fine dust. World-honored

One, the great chiliocosm that the Tathagata has spoken about is not

a great chiliocosm [132] and that is what is called a great chiliocosm.

And why is this? If that great chiliocosm really existed, then it

would be a compound lakshana. [133] The Tathagata has said that

a compound lakshana is not a compound lakshana, and so it is

called a compound lakshana."

"Subhuti, that which is a compound lakshana cannot really be spoken

about, and yet ordinary people are attached to it and greedy about it." [134]

In this section, the Buddha describes the nature of all worlds. He touches briefly on the idea that all lakshana are really compound entities; each of them arises only as a result of many factors. This is probably the single most common way of explaining emptiness: first, choose some lakshana and contemplate that it arises only as a result of many causes and has many components; then contemplate that all these components and causes are changing; then contemplate that there is nothing whatsoever about the lakshana selected that is permanent, absolute, or unchanging; lastly, contemplate that all lakshana are like this.

31 Not Giving Rise to Belief in Lakshana

"Subhuti, if a person were to say, 'The Tathagata teaches a view

of self, a view of human beings, a view of sentient beings, and

a view of souls.' Subhuti, what do you say, has this person

understood the meaning of what I am saying?"

"No, World-honored One. This person has not understood

the meaning of what the Tathagata is saying. And why is this?

The World-honored One has said that a view of self, a view of

human beings, a view of sentient beings, and a view of souls is not

a view of self, a view of human beings, a view of sentient beings,

and a view of souls and so it is called a view of self, a view of

human beings, a view of sentient beings, and a view of souls."

"Subhuti, one who commits to highest complete enlightenment

should not give rise to lakshana of dharmas;[135] *and he should*

know all dharmas in this way, and he should view them like this,

believe them, and understand them like this. Subhuti, the

Tathagata says that that which is called a lakshana of a dharma is not a lakshana of a dharma, and so it is called a lakshana

of a dharma. "

This section is a summary. Though the Buddha makes some subtle shifts in his choice of words, his meaning should be clear to anyone who has carefully studied and contemplated the preceding sections.

32 Like Shadows, Like Bubbles, Like Dreams

"Subhuti, if a person performs an act of generosity by giving away

as many precious jewels as would fill illimitable eons of worlds, and

if a good man or good woman commits to the bodhisattva mind,[136]

and upholds as few as four verses of this sutra, upholds them, reads

them, chants them, and teaches them, his or her goodness will be

greater than that of the first person. And how should this sutra be

taught to people? By not grasping lakshana, by remaining immo-

bile[137] *in this consciousness.*[138] *And why is this?*

> *All conditioned dharmas*
>
> *are like dreams, like illusions,*
>
> *like bubbles, like shadows,*
>
> *like dew, like lightning,*
>
> *and all of them should be contemplated in this way."*

When the Buddha finished speaking this sutra, the elder

Subhuti, along with all the monks, nuns, upasaka, upasika, ashuras, and worldly and heavenly beings, heard what the Buddha

had said, and all of them were greatly pleased, and they all believed

it, received it, and practiced it.

Fittingly, this very powerful and concise teaching ends in verse. The Buddha says, "All conditioned dharmas are like dreams, like illusions, like bubbles, like shadows, like dew, like lightning, and all of them should be contemplated in this way."

"All lakshana are not lakshana, and that is what is called lakshana." The foundation of consciousness cannot be found among lakshana. It can be found only after all lakshana are seen to be evanescent, "like dreams, like illusions, like bubbles, like shadows, like dew." The contents of consciousness cannot be grasped, and thus, the foundation of consciousness is consciousness itself. "If you can see that all lakshana are not lakshana, then you will see the Tathagata."

Lest we become overly philosophical, the Buddha reminds us that good men and good women should commit to the "bodhisattva mind," for the goodness that comes from this is greater than that which comes from any material act whatsoever.

And how are we to convey this beautiful message to others? "By not grasping lakshana" and "by remaining immobile in this consciousness." *Immobility* is an attribute of the Tathagata, the Buddha, the enlightened mind. It means changeless, unconditioned, beyond lakshana, beyond cause and effect, beyond all phenomena, and thus it is the "base" or the "foundation" of all consciousness. How perfect that the *Diamond Sutra* ends with this thought linked to the context of sharing these truths with others. This statement is the Buddha's concluding answer to the question that first prompted the teaching contained in this sutra: "When good men and good women commit themselves to highest complete enlightenment, on what should they base themselves, and how should they subdue their minds?"

Due to its brevity, the significance of its message, and the marvelous intricacy of its structure, the *Diamond Sutra* stands practically alone among Buddhist sutras, and indeed among all of world literature. In this sutra, the Buddha clearly reveals his compassion and strength, as he teaches us the wisdom that will allow us to see through his eyes. Though this ultimate prajna teaching can be difficult to understand, it is more than worth the effort put into trying, for it provides us with the key to understanding life itself.

The sutra ends with the paragraph: "When the Buddha finished speaking this sutra, the elder Subhuti, along with all of the monks, nuns, upasaka, upasika, ashuras, all worldly and heavenly beings, heard what the Buddha had said, and all of them were greatly pleased, and they all believed it, received it, and practiced it." Just as all Buddhist sutras begin with the phrase "thus have I heard," so all of them end with a phrase that closely resembles this one. The presence of "upasaka, upasika, ashuras, all worldly and heavenly beings" in addition to "monks and nuns," indicates that this teaching is universal and that the universal consciousness that is the Buddha can be discovered by anyone. All we must do is try.

Notes

1. *Thus have I heard:* Though this phrase has become the standard in English, its literal translation is probably better; literally it means, "Like this I heard," or "I heard it like this." Among Buddhist sutras in general, it means that Ananda either heard the teaching himself or that a reliable person told him about it. In the case of the *Diamond Sutra*, it means that he heard it himself.

2. *Shravasti:* Also called Saheth-Maheth or Sauatthi. It was ruled by King Prasenajit.

3. *Jeta Grove:* The Jeta Grove was a summer retreat that was often used by the Buddha. Its full name is *Jetavana-anathapindasyarama*. It was given to the Buddha by Prince Jeta and Anathapindika.

4. *World-honored One:* One of the ten names of the Buddha.

5. *from house to house:* Literally, "begged in sequence" or "asked for alms in sequence." This connotes that the Buddha did not consider any one house to be better than any another. He went to each one in a state of perfect equanimity. This phrase does not mean that he went to many houses; he probably stopped only at three or four of them before his bowl was filled with his one meal of the day.

6. *straightened his mat:* Literally, "straightened his seat."

7. *Subhuti:* One of the Buddha's ten most important disciples. Subhuti was also the most advanced of the Buddha's disciples in his understanding of emptiness, the heart of the prajna teachings.

8. *bared his right shoulder:* A sign of honesty and respect in ancient India.

9. *Tathagata:* Literally, the "thus-come-one." One of the ten names of the Buddha.

10. *bodhisattva:* A compound word made up of two Sanskrit words—*bodhi* and *sattva*. *Bodhi* means "enlightened" or "enlightenment," and *sattva* means "sentient being." A bodhisattva is not a buddha, but a sentient being with some measure of enlightenment.

11. *commit themselves to highest complete enlightenment:* This means "vow to attain highest complete enlightenment, or buddhahood." This vow is cited many times in the sutra.

12. *highest complete enlightenment:* From the Sanskrit phrase *anuttara-samyak-sambodhi.* This is the enlightened state of all buddhas and the ultimate goal of all Buddhist practice.

13. *base themselves:* "Base" works well in this and in other contexts for the Chinese *chu.*

14. *subdue their minds:* This is a literal rendering. It means "subdue (*hsiang fu*) all defiled tendencies of the mind." This phrase has the sense of "defeating" them. Defiled tendencies (Sanskrit: *kleshas,* Chinese: *fan nao*) are all of the thoughts, beliefs, actions, impressions, dreams, fears, desires, intentions, and so on of an unenlightened mind. These tendencies are sometimes referred to as demons in other Buddhist texts, in which case, the same verb (*hsiang fu*) is used to describe defeating or subduing them.

15. *great bodhisattva:* Master Ching K'ung (b. 1927) has defined the term this way: "To be completely unattached is to have great wisdom. To be deeply generous is to have great compassion. When wisdom, compassion, vows, and practice all are great—this is a great bodhisattva."

16. *sentient being:* Any being with a mind. Sentient beings are usually thought of in Buddhism as conscious beings that do not understand the deep source of their awareness. Their ignorance causes them to suffer, and to reincarnate again and again. The *Avatamsaka Sutra* says, "A buddha is a sentient being who has realized that he is a buddha. A sentient being is a buddha who has not yet realized that he is a buddha."

17. *to be saved:* Literally, "attain extinction and crossing over," i.e., attain salvation or nirvana.

18. *nirvana:* Enlightenment. The extinction of all suffering and delusion. See Chapter 3, Part I for more detail.

19. *be they born of...will not perceive:* The gist of this is all manner of sentient beings without exception.

20. *lakshana:* This word is often translated as "mark," "sign," "thought," "concept," or "characteristic." See the commentary beginning on page 47 for a more complete explanation of this word. See also note 22.

21. *soul:* This could also be rendered as an "entity that lives for a long time,"

an "entity that perdures over time," an "entity that clings to life," or an "entity that reincarnates." See Chapter 3, Part II for a more complete explanation of this word.

22. *Subhuti, if a bodhisattva has lakshana of self, lakshana of human beings, lakshana of sentient beings, or lakshana of a soul, then he is not a bodhisattva:* In this line, the Buddha is categorically denying the validity of any and all "notions," "ideas, "concepts," "dreams," beliefs," "perceptions," "feelings," "thoughts," "concepts," or "senses" of self. The word *lakshana* includes all of these English words. Most of the rest of the *Diamond Sutra* is a continuing explication of this line. There is no short-hand English phrase that can capture all of its nuances without limiting it. Readers should be wary of thinking that there is. However, a possible summation might be "Subhuti, a bodhisattva who has even the slightest iota of self is not a bodhisattva."

23. *phenomenal world:* Literally, "within dharmas." The phenomenal world is everything that can be seen, heard, smelled, tasted, touched, felt, thought about, dreamed, imagined, or cognized in any way.

24. *generosity:* Generosity is a fundamental Buddhist virtue. It is the first of the six paramitas.

25. *without basing it on anything:* Without having any attachment to it or to the results of it. The word "base" (Chinese: *chu*) in this line is the same verb encountered in section two: "on what should they base themselves, and how should they subdue their minds?" Of that line, Chiang Wei-nung said, "The Buddhadharma is an active practice, not a passive base."

26. *form, sound, smell, taste, touch, and thought:* The six senses recognized in Buddhism are sight, sound, smell, taste, touch, and the thought processes that coordinate these. These are the basic perceptual elements of the deluded, phenomenal "self."

27. *generosity...should not be based on any lakshana:* "All lakshana are delusive." All of them are empty. To base any act on any lakshana is to create suffering. To base an act of generosity on lakshana is to distort the intention behind the act. The same verb that we have seen before (see note 25) is being used here.

28. *goodness:* Chiang Wei-nung said, "Goodness is perfect realization of the pure dharma body." Master Tz'u K'ung said, "Anyone who believes this sutra has goodness." See note 36 for a full explanation of *goodness.*

29. *in any direction:* Literally, "south, west, north, the four ordinal directions, up and down…"

30. *on this teaching and this teaching alone:* Literally, "only on this teaching." Because the emphasis is strong, the Buddha's meaning is expressed better by the longer phrase.

31. *bodily lakshana:* A very common interpretation of this passage is that the lakshana referred to here are the thirty-two marks of the *sambhogakaya*—the Buddha's transfigured body as apprehended by great bodhisattvas. Since the thirty-two marks are discussed in later sections of the sutra, it probably makes more sense to understand this passage as being concerned with the more basic lakshana associated with corporal form. Readers interested in the thirty-two marks may turn to Chapter 26 for a more complete discussion of them. "Can you see the Tathagata in his bodily lakshana" could also be rendered "can the Tathagata be seen in his bodily lakshana?"

32. *all lakshana are not lakshana:* Literally, "all lakshana are no-lakshana."

33. *I:* Literally, "Tathagata."

34. *pure moment of belief:* This is a deeper level of belief than the first mention of belief in the phrase "believe this teaching." This first kind of belief indicates that one "will have planted good roots…with tens of millions of Buddhas," while the second kind of "pure" belief leads to one actually being seen and known by the Tathagata.

35. *intimately:* Literally, "in great detail, intricately, completely."

36. *goodness:* The Chinese is *fu te*, which literally means "good fortune and virtue." Sometimes it is rendered as "merit." Since merit has so many implications that are superfluous to the deep import of the *Diamond Sutra* as a whole, the word *goodness* seems to be a better choice. The Hua-Yen school of Chinese Buddhism has a beautiful explanation of goodness. They say that there are two streams of dependent origination. One of them courses among defiled things, and in this stream the Tathagata is without power. The other stream courses among pure things, and in this stream the Tathagata is all-powerful. This explanation, though not complete, is quite appropriate to this use of the word *goodness*, for in this section it is used to refer to someone "being seen and known" by the Tathagata. Needless to say, *goodness* in this context has little to do with Western concepts of good and evil.

37. *even so little as:* This does not appear but is implied by the context.

38. *non-law:* Here, *law* is generally thought to refer to the Buddha's more basic teachings: the five *skandhas*, the eighteen realms, the twelve *nidanas*, and so on. "Non-law" is generally thought to refer to the Buddha's teachings on emptiness. In this section, the Buddha makes it very clear that neither of these teachings can be clung to and that, indeed, nothing can be clung to. The foundation of consciousness does not reside in the lakshana of the senses, or the lakshana of the mind.

39. *Has the Tathagata really spoken a Dharma?:* Or, "Does the Tathagata really have a Dharma to speak about?"

40. *dharma:* When spelled with a lowercase "d," *dharma* means anything that can be thought of or named. "Definite dharma" could also be rendered "absolute dharma."

41 *there is no definite Dharma:* Even the teachings of the Buddha are empty. This does not mean that they are not true, or that they are not valuable. This only means that they have no definite form.

42. *held onto:* Literally, "grasped," in the sense of clinging or being attached to.

43. *unconditioned dharmas:* The eight unchanging attributes of the Tathagata or the enlightened state. Since these attributes are qualities of the Tathagata, this line might be interpreted to mean "All bodhisattvas understand the Tathagata differently." The truth is one, but the angles from which we perceive it are different. Buddhist sutras generally agree that the unconditioned state of enlightenment is: (1) timeless, (2) without delusion, (3) ageless, (4) deathless, (5) pure, (6) universal, (7) motionless, and (8) joyful. The *Shu Ch'ao* says, "To not understand that both people and the Dharma are empty is to be attached [to something], while to understand that both of these dharmas are empty is to be 'unconditioned.'" Huang Nien-tzu says, "The deep truths of the Mahayana are the unconditioned dharmas."

44. *precious jewels:* Literally "seven precious," or "seven treasures." The seven precious jewels are gold, silver, lapis lazuli, glass, amber, pearls, and coral.

45. *great chiliocosm:* The Sanskrit for this term is *trisahasra mahasahasra lokadhatu.* A great chiliocosm is one buddha realm. It consists of a billion worlds.

46. *goodness:* Master Hui Neng said, "True goodness resides in the dharma body; it is not a reward."

47. *devoid of a 'goodness nature':* Goodness, too, is empty. Emperor Hsuan Tsung (713–55) said, "Though a great chiliocosm of precious jewels is a lot, it still is a finite amount, and it can be used up. Though four verses [of this sutra] are not much, if they are understood, they will lead to enlightenment."

48. *all buddhas and all highest complete enlightenment are born of this sutra:* Literally, "all buddhas and all highest complete enlightenment dharmas of all buddhas issue from this sutra." This is an emphatic way of saying that enlightenment comes from understanding this sutra.

49. *the Buddhadharma is not the Buddhadharma:* That is to say, the Buddha-dharma is empty, too.

50. *Would it be right for:* Literally, "can a…" or "would a…be able…"

51. *shrotapana:* "Stream-enterer" or "stream-winner." One who has entered the "stream of saintliness" and will reincarnate as a human or heavenly being only seven more times. The first of the four fruits.

52. *the fruit of:* Here, *fruit,* as in most Buddhist texts, means "result," in this case, the elevated consciousness that results from the practice.

53. *sakradagami:* One who will reincarnate as a human being only one more time. The second of the four fruits.

54. *no such thing as returning:* This might be expanded to read, "no such thing as returning, nothing to return to, and no one to return."

55. *anagami:* One who will not reincarnate as a human being any more. The third of the four fruits.

56. *arahant:* A "foe-destroyer," one who has attained nirvana. The fourth of the four fruits.

57. *clinging to self, human being, sentient being, and soul:* The verb in this phrase literally is "cling." Contrast this to "has lakshana of self," etc. This shows that when the Buddha says "has lakshana" he means "has" and not "be attached to" or "cling."

58. *I have attained:* It should be noted that Subhuti is not bragging here. He defers entirely to the Buddha's assessment of his progress. His answer exhibits a refreshing absence of false humility.

59. *nondisputational samadhi:* This state is called "nondisputational" because it is beyond all duality, and thus nothing can arise that will cause one to enter into a dispute. The *Avatamsaka Sutra* says, "That which is disputa-

tional refers to life and death, while that which is nondisputational refers to nirvana."

60. *aranya:* Literally, "forest dweller." Refers to certain ascetic and reclusive practices. "Takes delight in the practice of aranya" could also be rendered "one who takes delight in the practice of aranya."

61. *Dipankara Buddha:* Dipankara means "lamp lighter" or "kindler of lights." The first of the twenty-four buddhas who preceded Shakyamuni Buddha in this world. During the time of Dipankara Buddha, Shakyamuni Buddha was not yet a buddha; he was a bodhisattva. The examples he gives in this section more or less tell us how he thought and what he did before he became a buddha.

62. *magnificent:* This refers to the six paramitas: generosity, restraint, patience, diligence, meditation, and wisdom. The magnificence of a bodhisattva resides in his virtue. Master P'u Wan says, "Magnificence means purifying one's mind." Notice the parallelism with "gain anything by his practice of the Dharma." The Buddha, while he was himself a bodhisattva, did not "gain anything by his practice of the Dharma." Similarly, a bodhisattva does not make "a buddha realm magnificent."

63. *magnificent is not magnificent:* That is to say, true magnificence is beyond even the magnificent purity of pure virtue. There is no form, or thought, or mental construct anywhere that can fully describe it.

64. *what is called magnificence:* This might also be rendered, "this is what magnificence really means" or "this is the real meaning of magnificence."

65. *purity of mind:* The original, enlightened mind, the buddha within. It is not born, does not die, is independent of phenomena, and is beyond duality.

66. *Mount Sumeru:* The "world mountain" that stands at the center of a world system. It is surrounded by seas.

67. *would that body be large?:* Subhuti's answer reaffirms that there is no lakshana anywhere that possesses an absolute reality. Even a body as great as Mount Sumeru is "no body."

68. *large body:* Even if one had a body as large as Mount Sumeru, one should still "give rise to a mind that is not based on anything." The metaphor is appropriate to the expansion of awareness that results from giving rise to a mind that is not based on anything.

69. *precious jewels:* Literally, the seven precious jewels.

70. *should be honored:* At its most basic and important level *honoring* means "having respect and love for." The *Mind Imprint Explication* says that beyond this, there are ten material ways to honor someone or something: with plain incense, with flowers, with ornaments, with powdered incense, with perfume, with burning incense, with banners, with clothes, with music, and with palms pressed together.

71. *heaven:* One of the six realms of conscious existence. The heavenly realm is very pleasant.

72. *ashuras:* Ferocious beings who inhabit one of the six realms of conscious existence.

73. *and it should be honored as if it were one of his disciples:* The sentence is commonly rendered: "Wherever this sutra can be found, there also is the Buddha or one of his respected disciples." Unfortunately, this interpretation does not work well with Kumarajiva's translation since the word "respect" (Chinese: *tsun chung*) in the last clause is clearly a verb and not an adjective. This is one of the two or three clauses in the *Diamond Sutra* whose meaning will probably always be slightly uncertain. Another rendering is: "Wherever this sutra can be found, there also is the Buddha; and in that place he honors his disciples." Our uncertainty here may be due to the sutra's origin as part of an oral tradition. In that case, the concluding phrase would have referred only to someone reciting this teaching from memory, and thus, it is the speaker who "should be honored." *Disciples:* At a very basic level, anyone who studies the Dharma is a disciple of the Buddha. At a deeper level one becomes a true disciple of the Buddha only after one has shown one's intention to do so by taking refuge in the Triple Gem.

74. *the perfection of wisdom is not the perfection of wisdom and that is what is called the perfection of wisdom:* Although Kumarajiva's translation does not contain this line (his version does not have "…and that is what is called the perfection of wisdom"), all other early versions of this sutra do.

75. *seen:* This means "seen, known, or perceived." The Tathagata must be experienced to be known.

76. *marks:* This is the same word that we have left as "lakshana" in other contexts. Thirty-two marks is the usual translation. See Chapter 26 for an explanation of the thirty-two marks.

77. *generosity:* The generosity of this line is usually interpreted as sacrificing one's life for the good of other sentient beings.

78. *of all the wise things...:* Literally, "Since long ago when I attained the wisdom eye..."

79. *sutra:* It is unlikely that Subhuti would have actually called these teachings a "sutra" since a sutra is something that is written down. He probably would have said "these teachings" or "these truths."

80. *true lakshana:* (Chinese: *shih hsiang*) Here *lakshana* does not imply delusion. *True lakshana* is a synonym for "enlightenment". Master Ching K'ung said, "Highest complete enlightenment is the true lakshana of prajna."

81. *all buddhas:* This is a common phrase that essentially means "buddha mind." Ultimately "all buddhas" are one Buddha, the Buddha mind, the originally enlightened mind. In this case, the sentence means that the Buddha mind or the enlightened mind is not attached to or based on any lakshana.

82. *supreme paramita:* Prajna paramita, the perfection of wisdom. This paramita is the supreme paramita because only wisdom can tell us how to employ the other paramitas. Without wisdom, we might be patient when we should act, or generous to those with whom we should not be, and so on.

83. *real words, truthful words, correct words, not false words, and not one who changes his words:* Hsieh Ling-yun (385–433) said, "*Real* means not devoid of meaning, *truthful* means not fabricated, *correct* means in accordance with deep principles, *not false* means not lying, *not changing* means that they stay the same from start to finish."

84. *generous...with as many bodies as...:* The generosity of this passage means sacrificing for the benefit of others "as many bodies as there are grains of sand in the Ganges River." *Many bodies* is an imaginary possibility used to emphasize the difference between someone who sacrificed his life and someone who "heard this sutra, who believed it, and who did not go against it."

85. *an immense number of eons:* Literally, "an infinite and immense number of 1,000,000,000,000,000,000 eons." *Eon* is often translated as "kalpa"—a very long time period, whose actual length is unclear.

86. *great vehicle...supreme vehicle:* The "vehicle" of helping others as opposed to the lesser vehicle of helping only oneself.

87. *uphold:* Literally, "receive and uphold."

88. *should be the cause of the person falling into a lower realm:* The hell realm,

the realm of hungry ghosts, or the realm of animals. The clear implication is that upholding the *Diamond Sutra* has lessened the effects of the person's bad karma.

89. *before Dipankara Buddha:* "Before" in the sense of space, not time.

90. *countless Buddhas:* The actual number given is 32,000,000,000,000, 000,000 multiplied by either 10,000 or 100,000.

91. *billion billion:* The actual number is 10,000,000,000,000,000,000.

92. *Dharma-declining age:* An indeterminate age after the time of the Buddha, in which the Dharma is poorly understood and rarely practiced.

93. *deep doubts:* Literally, "fox doubts."

94. *give rise to a mind like this:* That is, have this sort of awareness, or develop this sort of consciousness.

95. *attainable dharma:* Could also be read as "a dharma by which highest complete enlightenment is attained."

96. *essence of all dharmas:* Might also be rendered as the "thusness of all dharmas," or the "suchness of all dharmas." Three other English words that bear some resemblance to this idea are "quiddity," "immanence," and "haecceity." "The essence of all dharmas" means that the Tathagata is in everything, but not of anything. He permeates everything, but is not conditioned by anything. "He" is the "nirvanic aspect," or the "enlightened aspect" of all things. "He" is the unique nowness of the eternal and universal oneness of all possible things.

97. *The Tathagata has attained...for the Buddha to attain:* This line shows that the words *Tathagata* and *Buddha* are used interchangeably in the *Diamond Sutra*.

98. *between these two:* Between being "the essence of all dharmas" and there being "no such thing as highest complete enlightenment." Since the Tathagata is in everything but not of anything, he is "between these two." Since he is in everything, he cannot be pinned down to any single dharma or group of dharmas; thus, his attainment is "neither true nor false."

99. *all dharmas are the Buddhadharma:* An old Chinese poem expresses this point well: "The yellow flowers outside my window all are prajna, as the bamboo growing in my courtyard all is Bhutatathata." On this point, Master Tao Yi once said, "From beginningless time, sentient beings have

remained within the samadhi of the phenomenal nature; they cling to the phenomenal nature, wearing clothes and eating food within it. They talk, make comparisons, use their senses, and do many things within the limits of the phenomenal nature. They do not understand how to return to the source, so they chase after names and lakshana, and become more and more confused, as they create more and more bad karma. If within the space of a single thought, they can see the light of truth reflected in themselves, then their beings will become saintly, and they will see that the Buddhadharma resides in everything, everywhere."

100. *it is the same as a person growing up:* A person changes as he grows up, yet in some ways he remains the same. The elusive meaning of "all dharmas" is like this. From a conventional point of view, it means one thing, while from the Tathagata's point of view, it means something else. All dharmas are always changing, and yet there is something about all of them taken together that remains the same; they all are the Buddhadharma; they all remain the "same person." Another very common interpretation of this line and the line that follows it is: "Subhuti, it is like a person's great body." Subhuti said, "World-honored One, the Tathagata has said that a person's great body is not a great body and that that is what is called a great body." In this case "great body" is usually interpreted to mean "Dharma body." Some commentators call this "great body" a "large body," which means a healthy, well formed, adult body; in this case this line is referring to the emptiness of even such a body. Other reasons for choosing the "growing up" interpretation for this line are: (1) the "great body" explanation was given in section ten; (2) the Chinese for "great" (in "great body") in this section is more naturally read as "growing up" (*chang ta*); and (3) the example makes better sense. The fact that some parts of the *Diamond Sutra* are open to more than one interpretation indicates how well the text has been preserved from ancient times, even as the precise meaning of some lines has become uncertain.

101. *when a person grows up:* The person who reaches adulthood is very different from the child that began life, and yet we think of him as the same person.

102. *he is not a bodhisattva:* Literally, "he is not called a bodhisattva."

103. *dharma of selflessness:* This means that nothing has a permanent or absolute self-nature; everything is empty.

104. *eyes of flesh:* Physical eyes. The *Avatamsaka Sutra* says, "Eyes of flesh see forms."

105. *heavenly eyes:* The eyes of heavenly beings and advanced meditators in the human realm. Heavenly eyes can see in the dark and have some psychic powers. The *Avatamsaka Sutra* says, "Heavenly eyes can see into the minds of sentient beings."

106. *wisdom eyes:* The eyes of a sage who understands the meaning of emptiness, but does not yet comprehend the importance of compassion. The *Avatamsaka Sutra* says, "Wisdom eyes can see all the roots of sentient beings."

107. *Dharma eyes:* The eyes of an advanced bodhisattva who understands both emptiness and the importance of having compassion for all sentient beings. The *Avatamsaka Sutra* says, "Dharma eyes can see that all dharmas are the true lakshana."

108. *buddha eyes:* The awakened eyes of an all-knowing buddha. The *Avatamsaka Sutra* says, "Buddha eyes can see [with] the ten powers of the Tathagata."

109. *"…has the Buddha said that the sand in the Ganges River is sand or not?":* This question, taken along with Subhuti's answer, could not be a clearer affirmation of the reality of this world. "Yes…the Tathagata has said that it is sand."

110. *gotten hold of:* The same Chinese word, *te*, that has elsewhere been translated as "attain." *Attain* does not convey the force of the Buddha's statement in this line. There is no absolute dharma called mind that can be found anywhere, neither in the past, the present, nor in the future. The Tathagata intimately knows all sentient beings because he is all of them.

111. *form body:* The Buddha's human body, his transformation body. In the phrase "complete form body," the word "complete" connotes "even the complete form body." This sentence means something like: "Even given the best case, even in his complete form body, even in the best of all possible form bodies can the Buddha be seen?"

112. *ought not to be seen:* The Buddha cannot be fully understood merely by looking at his form body. Even in the best case scenario, the Buddha "ought not" to be looked at in this way. Subhuti's answer is based on the assumption that the Tathagata cannot be seen even in the best of all possible form bodies.

113. *all complete lakshana:* This is a literal rendition. This phrase again connotes a best case scenario; it means, "Can the Tathagata be seen by any

possible lakshana or any possible combination of lakshana, even if these lakshana are perfect?" The answer to this question is no. This passage raises the one prior to it to a new level. The meaning of "all complete lakshana" is much more inclusive than "form body." Lakshana encompass far more than visual attributes.

114. *completeness of all lakshana:* There is no notion of "completeness" that is sufficient to confine the Tathagata within the realm of lakshana.

115. *never say...do not have that thought:* This is the most commanding tone the Buddha has used so far.

116. *the wise Subhuti:* This is the first time he has been called "wise." This word adds emphasis to the Buddha's assertion.

117. *not not sentient beings:* Following strict rules of Western logic, this double negative may seem either unnecessary or to cancel itself out. In the *Diamond Sutra* it means that sentient beings are neither sentient beings nor the lakshana of not being sentient beings. There is no lakshana whatsoever that can describe them, and "this is what is called sentient beings," (i.e., this is what sentient beings really are).

118. *not even the slightest dharma that can be attained in highest complete enlightenment:* Literally, "the slightest dharma that I can attain." Notice that there is "something" called highest complete enlightenment; it is just that not even the slightest dharma can be attained "in it" or "from it." It is an awareness with no definable coordinates.

119. *good dharmas:* These are moral acts that benefit sentient beings and do not harm them. As with every other positive term in the *Diamond Sutra*, good dharmas must not be reified. Chiang Wei-nung said that the essential purpose of the *Diamond Sutra* is to teach people how to "practice all good dharmas while going beyond all lakshana."

120. *billion billion:* The actual number given is 1,000,000,000,000,000,000.

121. *just so, just so:* Many commentators believe that Subhuti knew the right answer, but said what he did to help others see more deeply into the Buddha's meaning. This is a common interpretation of many questions asked of the Buddha in the sutras by his more advanced followers. This seems the most likely explanation here since in section thirteen, Subhuti answered the same question quite differently: "No, World-honored One. And why is this? The Tathagata has said that the thirty-two marks are not marks, and that is what is called thirty-two marks."

122. *wheel-turning sage-king:* A sage-king who keeps the wheel of righteousness turning throughout his reign also possesses thirty-two marks, and thus if the Tathagata can be "seen" (i.e. truly grasped) by his thirty-two marks, then he would be no different from a "mere" sage-king.

123. *consider this thought:* Literally, "if you have this thought."

124. *his lakshana:* Literally, "lakshana." At this level of awareness, the Tathagata is one with everything.

125. *attains...because his lakshana are incomplete:* Literally, this phrase means "attains highest complete enlightenment not due to lakshana being complete." There are other possible interpretations of this phrase, but they do not seem to lead into the Buddha's next statement or fit with the sutra as a whole as well as this one. In these closing sections, the Buddha is refuting the last remaining ways that these teachings could be misunderstood. In section twenty, he says that enlightenment could not be attained by "all complete lakshana." In the second paragraph of this section, the Buddha says that it cannot be attained by ending or extinguishing all dharmas. In the current sentence, the Buddha makes it clear that it cannot be attained by any incompleteness either. This interpretation assumes that an error has been made in the transmission of the text (*yi pu chu tzu hsiang* instead of *pu yi chu tzu hsiang*). There are three main interpretations of this line: (1) The one just mentioned. (2) The traditional Chinese one, which implies that the Tathagata does attain highest complete enlightenment because his lakshana are complete. This is explained as being an affirmation of "phenomenal" or "relative" reality and relies on a literal reading of the text. (3) The Tathagata does not attain highest complete enlightenment due to his lakshana being complete. This interpretation assumes that a mistake has been made in the transmission of the text and concludes that the Tathagata's attainment has nothing to do with completeness or perfection of lakshana, a point already made in section twenty. Readers are encouraged to decide this issue for themselves.

126. *the one who commits to highest complete enlightenment:* Anyone who wants to become a buddha must eventually commit to highest complete enlightenment. This phrase includes the Buddha himself but is meant to be an instruction to all who hear or read it.

127. *all dharmas are ended and extinguished:* Nirvana is often described as the "extinction" of all duality and all relative dharmas. At a certain level of awareness and practice, this is perfectly true. However, at other levels it is

not. The *Diamond Sutra* teaches an ultimate level of truth. In this sutra, the Buddha is teaching the emptiness of all dharmas, and thus he denies that there really is anything to be extinguished or ended. Ultimately "all lakshana are delusive," including the notion that any of them can or should be extinguished.

128. *lakshana are ended and extinguished among dharmas:* The appearance of the word *lakshana* here is an assertion of the basic vocabulary of this sutra. Dharmas are not extinguished, lakshana are not extinguished, and even lakshana among dharmas are not extinguished. The import of this passage is that nothing is extinguished.

129. *without self:* I.e., without self-nature, without any permanent or absolute aspect whatsoever.

130. *all bodhisattvas do not receive goodness:* Or "no bodhisattva receives goodness."

131. *collection of fine dust:* Literally, "grouping of fine dust." The Buddha speaks of a "grouping" of fine dust because this leads very naturally into the idea of compound lakshana, which follows. A grouping of fine dust is a good example of a compound lakshana.

132. *not a great chiliocosm:* This literally reads "not world." The Chinese for great chiliocosm is literally "three thousand great thousand worlds." *World* is used here as a short form of this phrase.

133. *compound lakshana:* A grouping, or convergence, or combination of lakshana. In a sense all lakshana are compound lakshana; that is one of the reasons they are delusive. Our perception of a book in our hands, for example, is a compound lakshana because that perception is comprised of the book, our hands, the reason we are holding the book, the room, the contents of the book, and so on. Subhuti does not need to explain any further why a compound lakshana is empty. The explanation given above was familiar to everyone who was present. The passage is again employing a best case scenario; if even a great chiliocosm is empty, then so must everything else be.

134. *are attached to it and greedy about it:* Literally, "are greedy and attached to this event," or "are greedily attached to this event," The word *event* (Chinese: *shih*, Sanskrit: *artha*) is the companion to the term *rational principle*, or *truth* (Chinese: *li*, Sanskrit: *siddhanta*). Use here of the word *event* connotes an explanation of the universe in which all dharmas are events that arise out of, or according to, a rational principle

that underlies everything. This active, changeable, event-like sense of what a "thing" really is, is fundamental to the teaching of the *Diamond Sutra*. Dharmas are delusive, in part, because they are always changing.

135. *lakshana of dharmas:* These two words are close in meaning. *Dharmas* are everything that can be named. *Lakshana* are dharmas closely associated with cognition or awareness. This phrase could also be read "a lakshana or a dharma."

136. *commits to the bodhisattva mind:* Not "commits to highest complete enlightenment" because, ultimately, highest complete enlightenment can only be found through the practice of compassion. This is one of the most important themes of the *Diamond Sutra*. The Buddha's shift in vocabulary here shows that he believes that this point has been made.

137. *immobile:* That is, neither changing, nor moving. Immobility is one of the eight aspects of the Tathagata.

138. *in this consciousness:* The Chinese (*ju ju*) literally means "like, like," or "thus, thus." This denotes the level of reality experienced by a Tathagata; remember the word *Tathagata* means "thus-come-one." The line "by remaining immobile in this consciousness" literally translates as, "thus, thus immobile." Huang Nien-tzu says that the second *thus* of this line means "the Tathagata." In this case, the line would read: "remain immobile like the Tathagata."

Glossary

alaya consciousness: (Sanskrit: *alayavijnana*. Literally, "storehouse consciousness") Often called the eighth consciousness or the container consciousness. It is the level of consciousness in which all karmic seeds are stored.

anuttara-samyak-sambodhi: (Literally, "highest complete enlightenment") This is the enlightened state of all buddhas and the ultimate goal of all Buddhist practice.

arahant: (Literally, "foe-destroyer") One who has attained nirvana.

Bodhidharma: (?–535 C.E.) An Indian monk who brought the Ch'an lineage to China. He is famous for his direct speech and for having spent nine years in retreat at Shao Lin Temple in Honan, China.

bodhisattva: (Literally, "one who enlightens sentient beings") It means (1) Anyone who is seeking buddhahood. (2) A highly realized being who stands on the edge of nirvana but remains in this world to help others achieve enlightenment.

Buddha: (Literally, "awakened one") There are innumerable buddhas in the universe. Shakyamuni Buddha is the historical Buddha who taught the Dharma on earth. He is generally thought to have lived between the years 463–383 B.C.E.

buddha nature: The enlightened essence of all things. All sentient beings have buddha nature. It is hidden from our awareness by greed, anger, and ignorance.

Buddhadharma: The teachings of the Buddha. See Dharma.

Chao Ming, Prince: (499–529) A devout Buddhist, his division of the *Diamond Sutra* into thirty-two sections is the traditional division used in China.

Ch'an: (Sanskrit: *dhyana*, Japanese: *zen*) Meditation or absorption. Also the name of one of the eight major schools of Chinese Buddhism.

Chao Chou, Master: (778–897) A Ch'an master famous for the many koans he composed. A koan is a short question or statement that helps people discover deeper layers of themselves.

Chi Tsang, Master: (549–623) An influential Buddhist writer and thinker, known especially for his *Commentary on the Middle View*. Many of his students also became distinguished writers and teachers.

Chiang Wei-nung: (1873–1938) Author of one of the great modern commentaries on the *Diamond Sutra*.

Chih Yi, Master: (538–597) The founder of T'ien T'ai Buddhism and one of the first great Chinese Buddhist scholars.

chiliocosm: (Sanskrit: *trisahasra mahasahasra lokadhatu*) A great chiliocosm is one buddha realm. It consists of a billion worlds.

Ching K'ung, Master: (1927–present) An influential modern Pure Land master.

dependent origination: The Buddha's most basic insight into the workings of the phenomenal universe. Dependent origination means that no phenomenon originates out of nothing, but that all phenomena depend on other phenomena to bring them into being. Also known as "conditioned arising" or "conditioned genesis" because all phenomena are conditioned by other phenomena.

Dharma: (Literally, "carrying, holding") The teachings of the Buddha, which carry or hold the truth.

dharma: (Literally, "thing") Dharma with a small "d" means anything that can be thought of or named. Close in meaning to the English word phenomenon. Dharmas can be mental events, the passage of time, the order in which things occur, the appearances of things, and so on.

dharma body: (Sanskrit: *dharmakaya*) Body of the Dharma, body of the great order) One of the three bodies of the Buddha. The other two are the transformation body and the reward body. This term is often used to indicate the unity of the Buddha with everything that exists.

dharma realm: (Sanskrit: *dharmadhatu*) The realm in which all dharmas arise and pass away.

emptiness: (Sanskrit: *shunyata*) The absence of any absolute or permanent aspect whatsoever. All phenomena are empty. Sometimes translated as "transparency" or "openness."

five precepts: The five basic moral precepts of Buddhism: no killing, no stealing, no lying, no sexual misconduct, no irresponsible use of drugs or alcohol.

five skandhas: (Literally, "heap") The five basic "heaps" of psycho-physical stuff that are the building blocks of a person. They are form, sensation, perception, mental activity, and awareness.

generosity: The first and most basic of the six paramitas, the urge to reach out to others and help them.

Hsiao Yao-weng: (1562–1649) Author of a commentary on the *Diamond Sutra.*

Hsieh Ling-yun: (385–433) An influential lay Buddhist, he was a founding member of the White Lotus Society and an editor of Buddhist translations into Chinese.

Huang Nien-tzu: A gifted modern Buddhist essayist and lecturer, he writes mainly on Pure Land themes.

Hui Hai, Master: (late T'ang Dynasty) A well-known Ch'an master, he is the author of the *Treatise on Sudden Enlightenment.*

Hui K'o, Master: (487–593) The second patriarch of the Chinese lineage of Ch'an Buddhism. He studied for six years under Bodhidharma.

Hui Neng, Master: (638–713) The sixth and last patriarch of the Ch'an school. Master Hui Neng is reported to have become enlightened after hearing a man recite the *Diamond Sutra* on a street corner.

Hung Jen, Master: (602–675) The fifth patriarch of the Ch'an school of Buddhism and an important Ch'an thinker. It was his influence that made the *Diamond Sutra* a centerpiece of Ch'an.

Jeta Grove: A summer retreat often used by the Buddha. Its full name is Jetavana-anathapindasyarama. It was given to the Buddha by Prince Jeta and Anathapindika.

karma: (Literally, "work, action") The universal law of cause and effect, according to which all intentional deeds produce effects. Good deeds produce good effects, while bad deeds produce bad effects.

Kumarajiva: (344–413) One of China's greatest Buddhist translators. His works, which are still read today, are distinguished by their clarity and their apparent simplicity. In addition to the *Diamond Sutra,* he also translated the *Lotus Sutra,* the *Vimalakirtinirdesha Sutra,* the *Amitabha Sutra,* and the very influential *Treatise on the Perfection of Great Wisdom,* among others.

Lai Kuo, Master: (1881–1953) A modern Ch'an master, he was an influential lecturer.

lakshana: (Literally, "mark, sign") A basic unit of delusion. Lakshana are generated by intentional acts. They include all aspects of deluded awareness, including perceptions, memories, dreams, emotions, ideas, thoughts, sensations, etc. See page 47 for a more complete discussion, as well as notes 20 and 22.

Lin Chi, Master: (?–867) An influential Ch'an master, remembered most of all for exhorting his disciples to find the "true person" within themselves.

Mahayana: (Literally, "great vehicle") Buddhist practice dedicated to helping all sentient beings achieve enlightenment. The predominant form of Buddhism practiced in China.

middle way, middle path: Informal synonyms for the teachings of the Buddha, who emphasized balanced living and the avoidance of all extremes.

nirvana: (Literally, "extinction") The extinction of all causes leading to rebirth. The ultimate goal of Buddhist practice. Nirvana is not annihilation, but rather a different mode of existence.

no self-nature: Having no essence or permanent aspect whatsoever. The Buddha taught that no phenomenon or being has a self-nature. See also emptiness and dependent origination.

paramita: See six paramitas.

parinirvana: (Literally, "total *nirvana*") The great nirvana of Shakyamuni Buddha. His death.

prajna: (Literally, "wisdom") The highest level of Buddhist wisdom.

P'u Wan, Master: A well-known commentator on the *Diamond Sutra*. He lived during the early years of the Ch'ing Dynasty (1644–1911).

reward body: (Sanskrit: *sambhogakaya*) The Buddha's "second body" or "body of delight." In this body, the Buddha experiences the joy of his enlightenment.

samadhi: (Literally, to "concentrate") A profound state of meditative equipoise.

samsara: (Literally, "journeying") The world of delusion in which we journey for many lifetimes.

sangha: (Literally, "crowd") The community of Buddhist monks and nuns.

sentient being: All beings with awareness or the potential for awareness. The Buddha taught that eventually all sentient beings will achieve buddhahood.

Shakyamuni Buddha: The Buddha of our world system. The historical Buddha who taught the Dharma on earth. He is generally thought to have lived between 463–383 B.C.E.

six paramitas: (Literally, "perfections," or "that which has reached the other shore") The six cardinal virtues of a bodhisattva: generosity, restraint, patience, diligence, concentration, and wisdom.

six realms: The six realms of existence: hell, hungry ghost, animal, human, ashura, and heaven.

soul: (Chinese: *shou che*) That part of a sentient being that clings to life or that perdures.

Subhuti: One of the Buddha's ten most important disciples. Subhuti was also the most advanced of the Buddha's disciples in his understanding of emptiness, the heart of the prajna teachings.

Sun Chien-feng: Modern author of *Explication of the Diamond Sutra.*

sutra: (Literally, " threads") That which is threaded together, the written records of the Buddha's teachings. Early sutras were sewn together.

Taking Refuge: Short for "Taking Refuge in the Triple Gem," the name of the act and the ceremony that makes one a Buddhist and a true disciple of Shakyamuni Buddha.

Tan Hsu, Master: (1875–1963) The forty-fourth patriarch of T'ien T'ai school. His autobiography is widely read.

Tao An, Master: (312–85) One of the first Chinese nationals to be ordained as a Buddhist monk, he was an effective teacher and had many students.

Tao Yi, Master: (709–88) Also known as Ma Tsu Tao Yi. He is the founder of the first large Ch'an monastery in China, built in what is now Jiangxi Province. His influence can be felt to this day in all Chinese Buddhist temples.

Tao Yuan, Master: (1911–88) An influential teacher who was famous for his ability to explain Buddhist sutras.

Tathagata: (Literally, "thus-come-one") One of the ten names of the Buddha.

three bodies: The three bodies of a buddha. These are his transformation or physical body, his reward body, and the dharma body.

three Dharma seals: Impermanence, absence of a self-nature, nirvana. One of the Buddha's most basic teachings is that all phenomena and all states of mind are stamped with all three of these "seals."

three poisons: Greed, anger, and ignorance. The sources of all delusion and suffering.

three truths: The synthesis of phenomenal reality and the emptiness of that reality. Called the "three truths" because this synthesis is composed of three fundamental parts: (1) phenomenal reality, (2) the emptiness of phenomenal reality, and (3) the union of these two.

T'ien T'ai school: One of China's eight major schools of Buddhism. T'ien T'ai Buddhism emphasizes balancing practice and study.

transformation body: One of the three bodies of a buddha. The physical body that he uses to teach the beings of the realm in which he has manifested.

Triple Gem: The Buddha, Dharma, and Sangha.

upasaka, upasika: (Literally, "ones who sit close by") Lay Buddhists. Upasaka are male and upasika are female.

unconditioned dharmas: The eight unchanging attributes of the Tathagata or the enlightened state. Buddhist sutras generally agree that the unconditioned state of enlightenment is: (1) timeless, (2) without delusion, (3) ageless, (4) deathless, (5) pure, (6) universal, (7) motionless, and (8) joyful.

World-honored One: One of the ten names of the Buddha.

Yao Shan, Master: (751–832) A Ch'an master who studied under Master Tao Yi, he is remembered for having been a very good Buddhist scholar.

Yung Chia Hsuan Chueh, Master: (665–713) A Ch'an master who was a highly accomplished meditator. He is reported to have become enlightened after being questioned one night by Master Hui Neng.

Suggested Further Reading

Being Good: Buddhist Ethics for Everyday Life. Master Hsing Yun, Weatherhill, Inc., Trumbull, CT, 1999.

Buddha Nature. Sallie B. King, State University of New York Press, Albany, NY, 1991.

Buddhism Plain and Simple: Eight Realizations of Great Beings. Master Hsing Yun, Weatherhill, Inc., Trumbull, CT, 2001.

Ch'an and Zen Teaching, Volume 1,2,3. Lu K'uan Yu (Charles Luk), Samuel Weiser, Inc., York Beach, ME, 1993.

The Compass of Zen. Seung, Seung Sahn, Hyon'gak, Shambhala Publications, Boston, 1997.

The Conscious Universe: Parts and Wholes in Physical Reality. Menas C. Kafatos, Robert Nadeau, Springer-Verlag, London, 1999.

The Diamond Sutra: Transforming the Way We Perceive the World. Mu Soeng, Wisdom Publications, Boston, 2000.

The Diamond Sutra & The Sutra of Hui-neng. Translated by A. F. Price & Wong Mou-lan, Shambhala Publications, Boston, 1990.

The Diamond That Cuts Through Illusion. Thich Nhat Hanh, Parallax Press, Berkeley, CA, 1992.

Elaborations on Emptiness: Uses of the Heart Sutra. Donald S. Lopez, Princeton University Press, NJ, 1998.

The Emptiness of Emptiness: An Introduction to Early Madhyamika. C. W. Huntington, Jr., Geshe N. Wangchen, University of Hawaii Press, HI, 1995.

A General Explanation of the Vajra Prajna-paramita Sutra. Master Hsuan Hua, Translated by the Buddhist Text Translation Society, Dharma Realm Buddhas Association, Inc., San Francisco, CA, 1974.

Lotus in a Stream: Essays in Basic Buddhism. Master Hsing Yun, Weatherhill, Inc., Trumbull, CT, 2000.

Meditation on Emptiness. Jeffrey Hopkins, Elizabeth Napper (Editor), Wisdom Publications, Boston, 1996.

Only a Great Rain: A Guide to Chinese Buddhist Meditation. Master Hsing Yun, Wisdom Publications, Boston, 1999.

Perfect Wisdom, The Short Prajnaparamita Texts. Translated by Edward Conze, Buddhist Publishing Group, Devon, England, 1973.

Realizing Emptiness: The Madhyamaka Cultivation of Insight. Gen Lamrimpa, Translated by B. Alan Wallace, Ellen Posman, Snow Lion Publications, NY, 1999.

The Sutra of Hui-Neng, Grand Master of Zen: With Hui-Neng's Commentary on the Diamond Sutra. Translated by Thomas Cleary, Shambhala Publications, Boston, 1998.

Trance: From Magic to Technology. Dennis R. Wier, Trans Media, Ann Arbor, 1996.

Unlocking the Zen Koan: A New Translation of the Zen Classic Wumenguan. Translated by Thomas Cleary, North Atlantic Books, NY, 1997.

Zen and the Sutras. Albert Low, Tuttle Publishing, Boston, 1999.

About the Translator

Tom Graham has been doing Chinese studies for over twenty-five years, ten of which he spent living in East Asia. He has translated for numerous publications, and has worked on two other books with Master Hsing Yun: *Being Good: Buddhist Ethics for Everyday Life* and *Only A Great Rain*. He lives in San Diego, California.

About Fo Guang Shan

The Fo Guang Shan Buddhist Order and its affiliated temples and educational institutions in the International Buddhist Progress Society (IBPS) and the Buddha's Light International Association (BLIA) were founded by Master Hsing Yun and follow his nonsectarian teachings of Humanistic Buddhism. The United States headquarters for Master Hsing Yun's activities are at Hsi Lai Temple near Los Angeles.

Humanistic Buddhism affirms that the Buddha was born in this human world, cultivated himself in this human world, was enlightened in this human world, and taught beings the way to experience nirv›°a in this human world and not apart from it. Humanistic Buddhism teaches that we can live in the world fully and practice Buddhism at the same time. Humanistic Buddhism encourages us to integrate the Buddha's teachings of tolerance, loving-kindness, compassion, joyfulness, and equanimity into our lives for our benefit and for the benefit of all beings.

To learn more about Humanistic Buddhism and the activities of Master Hsing Yun, please contact:

Hsi Lai Temple
3456 South Glenmark Drive
Hacienda Heights CA 91745 USA
Phone: (626) 961-9697
hsilai.org
info@hsilai.org

Also Available from Wisdom Publications

Only A Great Rain
A Guide to Chinese Buddhist Meditation
Master Hsing Yun
Translated by Tom Graham
Introduction by John McRae

Essence of the Heart Sutra
The Dalai Lama's Heart of Wisdom Teachings
His Holiness the Dalai Lama
Edited by Thupten Jinpa

The Diamond Sutra
Transforming the Way We Perceive the World
Mo Soeng

The Lotus Sutra
A Contemporary Translation of a Buddhist Classic
Translated and Introduced by Gene Reeves

About Wisdom Publications

Wisdom Publications is the leading publisher of classic and contemporary Buddhist books and practical works on mindfulness. To learn more about us or to explore our other books, please visit our website at wisdompubs. org or contact us at the address below.

Wisdom Publications
199 Elm Street
Somerville, MA 02144 USA

We are a 501(c)(3) organization, and donations in support of our mission are tax deductible.

Wisdom Publications is affiliated with the Foundation for the Preservation of the Mahayana Tradition (FPMT).